T0381051

*A Woman's
Journey to Freedom*

THE BIG,
BROWN
SUITCASE

PARVIN KOLAHDOOZ

BALBOA.PRESS
A DIVISION OF HAY HOUSE

Balboa Press books may be ordered through booksellers or by contacting:

Balboa Press
A Division of Hay House
1663 Liberty Drive
Bloomington, IN 47403
www.balboapress.com
844-682-1282

Because of the dynamic nature of the Internet, any web addresses or links contained in this book may have changed since publication and may no longer be valid. The views expressed in this work are solely those of the author and do not necessarily reflect the views of the publisher, and the publisher hereby disclaims any responsibility for them.

The author of this book does not dispense medical advice or prescribe the use of any technique as a form of treatment for physical, emotional, or medical problems without the advice of a physician, either directly or indirectly. The intent of the author is only to offer information of a general nature to help you in your quest for emotional and spiritual well-being. In the event you use any of the information in this book for yourself, which is your constitutional right, the author and the publisher assume no responsibility for your actions.

Any people depicted in stock imagery provided by Getty Images are models, and such images are being used for illustrative purposes only.
Certain stock imagery © Getty Images.

Print information available on the last page.

ISBN: 979-8-7652-5311-3 (sc)
ISBN: 979-8-7652-5313-7 (hc)
ISBN: 979-8-7652-5312-0 (e)

Library of Congress Control Number: 2024911601

Balboa Press rev. date: 06/25/2024

I dedicate this book to all the girls and women on their path to freedom.

Contents

Hostage

The future belongs to those who believe
in the beauty of their dreams.
—ELEANOR ROOSEVELT

My heart races with anticipation as I step off the bus haphazardly, clinging to my only fortune at the moment. My big, brown suitcase symbolizes what life beyond holds for me. I feel invigorated as I scramble away from a group of people. I look back, and the bus disappears, a cruel reminder that "you are on your own, kid."

My tight grasp on Big Brown doesn't waver as I get pushed along. I find myself being sandwiched among a mass of people—caught up in a crowd that ensues chaos doesn't help my rising stress level.

I quickly disentangle myself from a multitude of men, carefully easing my way out so I don't end up touching any of them because that would land me in a problem I am in no mood to take on. Hence, I push on with all my gathered willpower and hopes for a better future.

I feel lightheaded and shaky as I march toward the embassy. I can feel the heat radiating from my body, yet my hands and feet run cold. The little rocks I feel under my feet propel me to drag my feet faster. As soon as I pick up my pace, the mass erupts in a sudden chorus of chants, which remains inconsequential to me as I almost lose my grip on my suitcase.

I look around, and it dawns on me how unrecognizable my country looks after the revolution. The air that once promised a new day full of opportunities accompanied by a brazen breeze of independence is now officially contaminated. The stench of sweat and the foul smell of smashed, rotten fruits scattered around the footpath as if stomped on, with overflowed garbage bins everywhere, reminds me that Iran will never be the same again.

It has almost been a year since the revolution struck us in full force and made the civilians' lives, especially those of women, a living hell. So much has happened in the past year that we, as a collective society, have become accustomed to the chaos.

Events leading up to this crucial decision of mine weren't abrupt. It has been the result of me undergoing a process of change and battling many internal wars, and then ultimately giving in and accepting the new reality set out for women by the government of the Islamic Republic of Iran in such a short span of time.

The grim revolution commenced in the winter of 1978, and the political and religious agendas took seed, sowing animosity among the masses for years to come—but Iran wasn't always like this.

It was mainly accustomed to peace under the rule of Mohammad Reza Pahlavi, also known as the shah of Iran. His leadership became a subject of political fluctuation, and further uncertainty ensued when his continuous monarchy was targeted. Despite turbulence in his government, his era granted a taste of liberation.

Shah wasn't exactly the prime example of effective administration and excellence, but he allowed cultural freedom. He pushed the country to be more secular and expanded educational opportunities for everyone.

Inequality among the sexes was an issue since the beginning, but by law women weren't subjected to such harsh treatment under his regime. They were allowed to dress however they wanted, could travel and visit places alone, had a right to vote, had a right to pursue any career path they wanted, and could marry whomever they liked whenever they deemed it right. They were not subjected to objectification and heinous loss of autonomy and social rights that prelude many aspects of their enjoying an individualistic life. To put it simply, they were not caged.

Many religious members of society weren't happy with his adoption of Western ideologies. They believed it threatened their religious sentiments and harmed the Islamic sanctity of this nation. That, along with many external factors, deemed him an unfit ruler, which led to the shah's monarchy collapsing. His government faced rebellious action by the opposition, which led to a terrifying insurgent uprising among the people.

I was in grade twelve, my last year of high school, when I first sensed the terror. I remember the day vividly. That's when everything went south. It was an early winter afternoon when I was walking home after school. I was so captivated by the chilly breeze that played with my hair and the warm ray of sunshine that danced around the canvas of my face from far away. I walked and walked, lost in my headspace, daydreaming. Suddenly, I was startled by the sound of heavy metal grinding against metal coming from down the street, but what drew my attention was the brutal screams coming from the same direction.

I hesitantly followed the unusual sound. My jaw dropped to the ground, and my senses sharpened from all the noise when I saw large army tanks on the roadside—hundreds of soldiers marching down Nader Street. Their aura created fear in people on the street as they maneuvered with machine guns in their hands.

I had never witnessed anything remotely like this. I felt a rising tide of fear from head to toe. Nader Street was a quiet block, mainly a residential street filled with houses, schools, other educational institutes, and a few stores and shop vendors on the corner that would light up at night. It was a quiet, friendly neighborhood. Parents felt safe enough to let their children play on the streets, kids raced with their bicycles, and girls played their imaginative games. They skipped ropes and told funny stories to each other. It was an ideal neighborhood to raise a family.

Seeing a pleasant neighborhood like Nader turned upside down was a devastating sight. Each step the soldiers took resonated heavily as they marched. The colossal metal treads of the army tanks crushing the new asphalt pavement sent shivers down my spine.

I watched the horror unfold from the corner of the street. The thunderous rumbling of the tanks echoed everywhere. I only took a minute to glance back at the screaming civilians. I could see their terror-stricken faces as they sought protection. Distress was evident in the way they scurried about the street. The vendors were in a hurry to close their shops. Women on the streets were rushing to reach home safely after work.

A palpable sense of anguish was in the air that day that fear-stricken people struggled to navigate. The constant disruption and overpowering army tanks made their efforts futile. The chaos doubled with each passing moment. I felt paralyzed. My feet stuck to the pavement until a group of people sprinted by without clear direction. One of them stumbled into me, which was my last straw. Their eyes reflected fear when they collected their loved ones into their arms and ran.

With a sinking feeling, I finally managed to race toward home. I gasped for air when I reached my house. As a seventeen-year-old, I had so many questions running wild in my mind. *Why are there soldiers and tanks on the streets? What had happened? Why were the civilians so terrified of them?*

I wouldn't call myself ignorant, but I was blissfully unaware of the grave situation my country was in due to the political uprising. I partially blamed myself for not being up-to-date with the current environment.

The scene on Nader Street plays in my mind on a loop, and I realize how much it looked like a warzone or one of those military movies you see on television. It had taken me a while to discover that the maneuvering was an attempt by the shah's army to demonstrate their strength and quell the pro-Khomeini people who had started the riot. The opposition rebelled against the current government, which created a revolutionary movement against the shah.

As a group of people walk past me, I am snapped out of these past memories. The people gathered around here are in a rush to get their hands on American visas as well. They are easy to distinguish among the extremists because of the way they are pacing around. Their lost, puffy eyes dart around, looking for answers. The melancholy and worry etched on their wrinkled faces is telling me everything I need to know; like me, they, too, are holding onto the ropes of freedom waiting to climb up. I walk past an elderly couple who has newspapers rolled up in their hands and a black suitcase with them.

They remind me of a much simpler time. How much my father was obsessed with papers and the news. He was hooked on listening to BBC World News and reading the paper every morning and evening.

During my elementary schooling, my father crafted an unusual ritual. Each evening, after the remnants of our dinner had been cleared, he would present me with the great Persian poet Hafiz's book or the daily newspaper. Even though my young heart harbored a profound aversion to the news, especially the mind-numbing political pieces, the ritual held a special place in my heart.

My father, a man who seldom wore his emotions on his sleeve, used this shared reading as a clandestine means of bonding. Our ritual wasn't merely about parsing the day's happenings. It was his silent declaration of love, his way of weaving moments of quality into the fabric of our lives.

His sweet voice used to echo through the house when he would call out for me. He would holler, "Parvin, *dokhtaram* [my daughter], read me today's, will you?"

"Coming, *Bābā*," I would reply as I ran down the stairs. I used to abandon everything I was doing at that moment to attend to him. Subconsciously, I was always seeking his approval and attention. His scent is still fresh in my mind. He smelled of cigarettes most of the time, and the warm embrace of his aftershave protected and comforted me.

When I'd finish reading the newspaper to him, I would notice his weary expression, his brows knit together, a gloomy look in his eyes. Sometimes, he'd interrupt me in the middle to ask if I understood what it all meant. I would shake my head no.

"Do you know what registry means, Parvin?"

"*Na, Bābā.*"

"The economic crisis has begun, my child; Iran won't ever be the same again," he said this one time.

It was as if I could comprehend what economic crisis meant at that age, but those words stuck with me because he was right even in those moments of obliviousness.

My father is no longer with us to witness everything that's been going on recently. He passed away six years ago, but if he were here with us now, maybe things wouldn't have gotten this hard for us. What I witnessed at Nader Street looked a lot like what I had read in the newspapers all those years ago to my dad about the warzone in Palestine.

After that day, people started living in fear, and Nader Street became unusually quiet. People were scared to send their children out to play. I barely saw kids going to school. Thousands of people rallied at that time. Riots would occasionally break out in the name of Khomeini fighting Shah's people. A lot of ongoing protests were disturbing the daily lives of civilians.

To our surprise, things got worse when pro-Khomeini riots intensified to a greater degree—frequent uproar and protests led by people involved religious clergy with bizarre slogans; young, poor, urban men with banners; and Shia women with their kids lifted upon their shoulders holding Ayatollah Khomeini's posters in their little hands, depicting him as the revered religious figure for Muslims. These demonstrators were determined. We could see the rage on their faces as they marched with bloodshot eyes, driven by the desire for political change and the rise of the Islamic establishment. These protests soon took a violent and disturbing shift, which led to a loss of life.

One of the prime reasons Ayatollah's demonstrators opposed Shah was because they were led to believe that his "Western agenda" was ruining the country. The sheer control women had over their lives and their bodies was somehow unacceptable to them. They wanted secularism to end, so to retaliate, they would often get on rooftops chanting, "*La elaha elallah, Khomeini rahbar*" (God is great; Khomeini is our leader).

More roaring slogans included "death to Shah" and "independence, freedom, Islamic Republic."

Unfortunately, Ayatollah's influence spread like wildfire among the masses, officially toppling the shah's autocratic leadership. Newspapers announced that he fled to another country with his family. I have a clear recollection of that day. I felt defeated, like I had lost my father all over again. It was one of the saddest days of my life. That's how everything in the country went downhill from there.

Ayatollah Khomeini rose to power right after the shah's exile, and the first thing he did, to no one's surprise, was to bring in the Islamic revolution. He immediately overthrew the shah's regime and established an Islamic Republic. After that, Iran's political, social, and economic ideologies took a drastic turn and started to impact international relations.

Khomeini's government promised quite a few things to the public, like free healthcare and free utilities, so most of the people were pleased with these assurances—or at least, that's what we thought. These promises were never met. My mother beamed with joy upon hearing such bold claims, and for my family, hearing such promises revived lost hope. I was still struck with grief and spent most of my days pondering the horrific possibilities his leadership would impose on civilians.

To no fault of her own, my mother believed that he brought a new ray of hope that families like us, middle-class households that were not fully financially equipped, would be cared for by the new government. I understood where she was coming from. My father's demise and the financial instability that followed had rattled our world. All the household responsibilities fell on her shoulders. Tragically, Khomeini failed to keep his word, which gave me a sense of bleak satisfaction that his government was as disappointing as I had predicted.

Moreover, the situation progressively declined, especially for women living under his regime. Riots, chaotic protests, and brawls became a part of our lives. Women had to cautiously sneak out of their homes to get an education or go to work to avoid getting attacked or sent home. Under Shah's rule, the *hijab* was optional; some women chose to observe, and some didn't, but soon after his regime ended, women started losing their bodily autonomy. Shortly, the women who had never worn a *hijab* were forced to comply. It escalated to the point that one of my acquaintances was even jailed for months for not adhering to the Islamic dress code and not observing the *hijab* properly. Women were living in constant trepidation.

I still remember the time when my mother and I were cooped up in our house for days. I was scared to leave the premises of my own home. We felt restrained from performing the simplest tasks that required us to be outside the house. I remember those panic-filled days when we couldn't even clean our windows because that required us to step outside. My mother and I shared a love for cleanliness and keeping our place neat. There wasn't a time in my life when we ignored the disheveled state of our house. We'd always be so quick to wash, scrub, sweep, and dust every nook and cranny of our home, but then came a time when our windows were smudged with dirt and grease smeared all over, which turned them black. We couldn't do anything about it because, as women, it was considered reprehensible for either of us to step outside for all the neighborhood to see, especially from homes that didn't have a patriarch.

Since we had no man at home, the windows stayed dirty for as long as we could remember. The point is how the basic livelihood of women was stripped away. They weren't allowed to have a proper conversation with men. Working women faced many hurdles in occupational settings. Many industries and firms would deny them jobs due to their Islamic constitution or to save face. Women who were already working were forced to resign. The ratio of women on the streets doing the most mundane things like grocery shopping or riding a bicycle started declining shortly afterward. Women were segregated and excluded in all spaces, treated like an afterthought—like a minority. Restrictions were placed regarding opportunities and autonomy; if these rules were defied, we were penalized and not just charged fines. The Islamic Republic government used other means of inhumane reinforcements to put women in their "place." Whipping and flogging were introduced as means of punishment. Depending on the severity of the charges held against them, up to seventy-four lashes was deemed fit for women who disobeyed the Islamic dress code rules set by Khomeini's government.

In short, women were made to understand that they were inferior to men, that they must avoid giving men any reason to abuse or punish them, and that they must fear the power men held over them.

Meanwhile, no corresponding harsh restriction was applied to men. Their freedom was not compromised, like ours. Many men appreciated Khomeini's government solely because it gave them an excuse and enabled their uncouth behaviors to take control over their women. It became easier for men to hide their insecurities under Khomeini's rule and incompetence behind patriarchy.

Under his rule, we learned many things about his government. Anyone who rebelled against his strict ideologies met their fate. He started executing people who stood in his path, sometimes in public—claiming them to be the enemies of his Islam.

As a religious supreme leader, he maintained a reputation for being inclined toward Islam only. That led to minority rights being removed. Religious minorities soon found it hard to practice their religions under his government. I started noticing religious minority groups felt the need to lay low because the people who followed Khomeini were known to be aggressive toward marginalized religious groups.

I recall the instances where minorities would often hide themselves for their safety. I have witnessed how scared religious minorities were at that time and still are. Jews, Christians, and Bahai people were tear-gassed and harassed if they were seen practicing their religious duties outside in public. Bahai houses were burned, looted, and trashed by pro-Khomeini followers, which instilled a newfound fear in me.

Daunting memories continue to cast a dark shadow on my present. As I drag my big, brown suitcase with me, I feel the weight of past circumstances heavy on my shoulders. My palms are sweaty, but my grip on my suitcase is still firm. When I see a couple before me, I imagine they, too, are here for a visa. They are looking around in bewilderment. What catches me off guard is how young the girl looks compared to the guy. She is covered from head to toe, with only her face visible, while her much older husband holds their documents.

Out of all the things the Khomeini government introduced, early marriages and polygamy were two rigid policies of his that he wanted women to adhere to. The state of Iran stooped so low to the point that marriage became the only option, indeed deemed the purpose of a woman's life. Women's individuality was utterly wiped out. It alarmed me the most to see all the capable, young, teenage girls in their prime getting wed to men twice their age. It was scary to see so many young women being vetted in front of families like a prized possession to sell. I was subjected to this horror too.

I remember the house was squeaky clean when a potential suitor's family came to see if we were a good fit.

I wore my pretty red dress that day and made myself look presentable. I washed my hair, brushed it to the side, and plastered on a fake smile as I walked into the room with a tray of tea and sweets. In front of me sat a young man, his parents, and a few other women. Ironically, this was the only time it was all right for a strange man to see me without a *hijab* at home, so they could deem me fit enough for their "standards." I remember being scared and anxious as I placed the tray before them, and they were staring at me in critical judgment. Their harsh facial expressions and holier-than-thou attitude was suffocating. I felt like an item at the grocery store being passed on to the man and his family, so the very idea of spending the rest of my life with this strange man terrified me to my core. Fortunately, we weren't meant to be together. Thank God.

However, my sister was not lucky enough to escape her fate. It broke my heart in a million pieces watching my beautiful, brilliant sister forced out of school and given away at fourteen to marry a man she didn't want, settle as a housewife, and raise children right after. That way of living would have been a slow death for me. This was when I started dreaming about freedom, which could not be attained if I stayed in Iran.

9

In the name of modesty, stronger restrictions started getting implemented. Veils and tent-like *chadors* were introduced as a mandatory dress code; one strand of hair on display or skin showing through the clothing was met with immediate consequences. All women and girls over eight were forced to obey these rules. I had to ensure my safety first before I could seek my freedom. I started covering myself early on, so that the men wouldn't inflict horrors upon me or see the shape of my body, which would cause their arousal.

Paradoxically, some men didn't leave women alone even if they were covered from head to toe, and they would still find a way to sexually assault or harass them on the streets. That's when I realized it had nothing to do with clothes and everything to do with power.

My daydreaming comes to a halt when I feel an unexpected crunch beneath my feet. I glance down instantly and realize I am stepping on a wrecked and charred book. I quickly step away. After a second, I reach toward it and place it right beneath a tree. Books are highly valued in my culture and not to be stepped upon. Education, overall, has always been considered a priority in Iran. Under Shah's rule, at least women were encouraged to pursue degrees and career paths.

I remember that before the revolution succeeded, my good friend Fahi was one of those whose passion was to become a teacher. She had enough patience and creativity to teach. It was on one of those cloudy days that I happened to tag along with Fahi, taking the bus downtown, where the *Sepahe Danesh* Ministry of Education was located, so she could apply to become a registered teacher. We were motivated that day because Fahi was about to do something for herself. She was prioritizing her needs. She chose a path that allowed her to be financially independent, giving me hope to pursue my own needs.

As the bus got closer to downtown, my heart started sinking for some reason as I gazed outside and saw heaps of people in the street, so much more crowded than usual, and from my personal experience, this kind of crowd always brought bad news. I looked around some more as I grabbed my friend's hand.

"You think it is safe to be here, Fahi? It is martial law, and yet so many people are out here," I asked for her reassurance.

"Oh, don't worry about it; we will be fine. It is just busier than usual today." She tapped my hand. Her carefree attitude and eagerness to apply both elevated and comforted me.

"All right," I sighed. "Let's just hope nothing goes wrong." I exhaled, but my eyes still darted out the window cautiously.

We stepped off the bus and walked toward the ministry. My chest tightened in a knot again when I saw soldiers with their guns on the street. I kept my gaze on the ground so I didn't end up looking them right in the eye.

We stepped inside the ministry building with our heads tilted down, trying to walk as fast as possible. Strangely, the ministry was more relaxed and less crowded, and the building blended classic architecture with a sophisticated Iranian touch to its work. The place exuded authority and dignity. Our footsteps echoed on the marble flooring as we marched forward. The atmosphere was lovely; we saw vibrant, smiling faces, and a sense of relief washed over us.

Fahi looked ecstatic. "I can't believe I am finally doing this," she said with the biggest smile. Seeing her this happy made me feel proud of her choices too.

"I am happy for you, Fahi."

We stood in line. Before too long, she applied to become a teacher, and we walked out. As soon as we stepped outside, the warm embrace of the ministry left, and the sinking feeling returned when I saw soldiers marching before us, scattering civilians in all directions screaming, *"marg bar shah"* (death to Shah), fear and panic evident in their eyes. The extreme level of distress in their body language was palpable, as terror and desperate need to reach home mirrored the chaos I witnessed on the streets of Nader months ago, resurrecting the same pain.

I was dumbfounded, and trauma struck once again; I felt frozen to the ground, not knowing what to do next. We tried to go back inside the ministry, but it was too late, and the gates were closed, so we had no option left but to return to the streets. To our bad luck, dread filled our hearts when we saw the soldiers running toward us, trying to scatter the demonstrators.

Before we knew it, a little canister of tear gas landed beside our feet and began spewing. The smog enveloped our surroundings, and our eyes instantly started tearing up. The smoke from the gas was so intense it overwhelmed me like nothing I had ever experienced before. My throat closed as Fahi began coughing, so we quickly stepped away and ran in the other direction. Our eyes were still closed, red, swollen, and irritated from the chemical.

It took us a solid fifteen minutes for the chemical to leave our body, and we could speak. "It's tear gas," Fahi enlightened me as she sneezed and coughed the tear gas out of her system.

"But we didn't do anything wrong," I said, still bewildered, unable to grasp what had happened.

"Let's get out of here. If they catch us, we will be in trouble." Fahi grabbed my wrist, and we made a run for it. We sprinted until we came across a spacious wooden staircase. "Here, let's hide under there for the time being."

We walked on our tiptoes like thieves and then kept our heads low as we crawled and crouched deeper under a dark staircase. The looming shadow of the staircase protected us and made us feel invisible for some time. The riot was not subsiding anytime soon. The soldiers were still hovering about the streets. I held my breath so my loud exhales wouldn't attract any attention. We kept hidden as we watched the uproar from the small holes between the wood planks of the staircase.

Our eyes were still watering from the residual tear gas in the air. I exhaled slowly. My heart felt like a little bird fluttering inside, collapsing, and trying to escape the cage. My mouth felt dry. The pungent odor of tear gas was unraveling in my system. The ground started spinning for me as I was bombarded with a sensory storm. It took us quite some time to simmer down from the effects. We kept quiet until we heard the soldiers' footsteps getting further away from our shelter.

We crawled out of the shadow and looked around to see if there was any sign of soldiers.

"They are gone," I whispered.

"Yeah, thank God. Let's go home," she said.

We ran as far as we could from that street and caught the bus. We were out of breath as we reached home. We glanced back at each other, rejoicing that we had made it alive.

Now, under the new regime, I have learned that our educational prospects were compromised too. Most women had only two options: either work as a teacher or get married. I rejected both because I was not interested in teaching or settling down and becoming a housewife. I was already seeing myself living a life far beyond those options.

I reflect on the significant events in my life that compelled me to make this decision. Now that I am standing on the pavement, staring from afar at the path that will lead me to the gates of the US Embassy, I think about all the young girls like me who couldn't flee and succumbed to their fate. I do not wish the same for me. No one deliberately wants to leave their homeland. Still, if the government becomes biased and starts inflicting pain on minorities and treating women like cattle in the name of religion, one feels the need to escape to where one will not be treated as such. I am startled when a vendor's loud voice reaches my ears. My grasp on Big Brown tightens as I pull her taut toward my legs. A part of me strongly believes that it's not me who carries my fortune in this suitcase, but rather my big, brown companion, which holds the resilience, endurance, and might that has escorted me to the gates of the US Embassy.

People are still rushing by as I stand still. Finally, a man notices and stops before reassuring me I am on the right path toward the American embassy. I realize the chanting is in the same direction. My heart sinks when I approach the noise. Some people run in the opposite direction, seemingly away from the embassy. Vendors with their merchandise on display are still trying to make a sale. The produce store beside the women's clothing displays his fresh fruits and vegetables. The aromas of freshly cut cantaloupe and watermelon in the air make my mouth water.

"Come and get it! Fresh herbs just brought in this morning," one vendor hollers.

"Latest style of clothing for women. Take a look. Good quality too." The second vendor's voice reaches my ears.

The crowd is thicker near the embassy. I can now hear people shouting, "Down with the USA." I have heard this chant a thousand times since the beginning of the revolution on January 7, 1978, and it still frightens me.

I raise my heels to see where the chanting comes from, but all I see are tall buildings. Maybe they are on the rooftop. I pay no attention to those chants and the shouting. I repeatedly tell myself I am there for a reason, and no amount of chanting and screaming will lead me astray from my long overdue freedom. The crowd is getting denser ahead. Everyone is surging to reach something. I am pushed and shoved around by the heaps of people, feeling like a grain of sand tossed by giant ocean waves. I remember my mother's warning.

"No girl from our family travels alone anywhere, let alone traveling to Tehran. Tehran is a busy, dangerous place for a girl. Why are you so hard-headed?" She has always opposed my independence, but I never blamed her because she, too, was conditioned. After all, when her lectures didn't work for me, she pulled out the religious repercussions of my decision.

"I am not happy with you, and you know what that means? This means God is not happy with you. You will not go to heaven when God is unhappy with you. So now, go do what you want to do."

I had heard these admonitions many times. They entered my head expecting to raise chaos, but they'd slide off the other side without getting a chance to do it. My dream was my only focus. I needed to get out of there. That was the only thing that played in my mind all those times leading up to my decision to visit the American embassy. Anything else was background noise trying to distract me from my goal.

I work my way through the crowd, feel my thigh pinched by a much older man, and wonder if my mother was right. What if I do get lost, kidnapped, or raped? How would I be able to manage everything alone? Each step gets heavier as doubts cloud my mind. I discard all the second thoughts from my mind and focus on one thing: my big, brown suitcase, which represents my freedom. My objective appears crystal clear, and soon I abandon all negative thoughts.

It's hard to see from a distance, but I can see something. This must be it—the American embassy. I think the crowd around the area must be people applying for an American visa. I hope there is no limit to the number of visas they are giving away; otherwise, I won't be able to get one by the time I get there. My eyes are pinned on the majestic, tall, black gates in the distance and the fence around the embassy. My heart pounds faster against my chest as I quicken my pace.

I am so close, but out of nowhere, a man on his bicycle pushes me over. I fall into Big Brown. The man yells, *"Khanom havaset kojast?"* (Where are you, girl?) And now he's asking, "How long must I ping the bell for you to hear me?"

I rise to my feet, ready to yell back at the person that I couldn't hear him, but a moment of déjà vu catches me off guard. As this has happened before, a weird wave of nostalgia washes over me and brings me back to my childhood. I watch the person on the bicycle disappear from my eyesight and realize how I haven't seen a single woman on a bicycle since the revolution.

I never had a bike growing up, either. Time after time, I was begrudgingly reminded that riding a bicycle was deemed only suitable for boys. Even my parents refused to buy me one.

However, at the age of sixteen, I started learning to ride a bicycle around my sister's yard. That bicycle belonged to my three-year-old nephew. The first time I learned to pedal, I fell and hurt myself, bruising my legs and arms, but that didn't stop me. I didn't give up until I was a pro at it, but all my efforts went down the drain because I was not allowed to ride outside the confines of my sister's yard. It was not permissible, and just when things couldn't get worse, the revolution happened exactly a year later, ruining my chances of riding a bike in the foreseeable future. That was my first realization of how unfair the world was to girls.

The chant gets louder as I continue to walk toward the embassy. *"Marg bar Amrica"* (down with America).

Even though it is November, the crowded street and people shoving and pushing me make it feel like a hot summer day. I can feel sweat dripping down my back and collecting beneath my *hijab*. I look around. I see a few other women around me fanning their faces with paper or fancy Japanese folding fans to relieve the heat under their layers of veil.

I'm not the only one suffering from the heat. My own body odor smells repulsive. I have been highly conscious of my appearance all my life, but today it matters less. I am here to get my visa, and that's all that matters.

I am standing so close to the gates of my freedom.

The noise is deafening: "Down with USA!" I have heard this chant a thousand times since the beginning of the revolution, and it still frightens me.

I ask a woman with a black *chador* and a *hijab*, covered head to toe, "What's happening?"

I can't hear what she replies.

I repeat, *"Che khabare?"* Moving close enough to her to hear her answer, I feel the heat projecting off her body.

She raises her hand and points to the gates with her index figure.

"*Gerogaan gereftim*" (We're taking hostages).

"What hostages?"

"*Aamricayeeha tooye sefarat*" (Americans in the embassy).

I don't understand what she is talking about. It's as if she's speaking a foreign language. I have never heard of the word "*gerogaan*" (hostage) before. I feel this rage coming over me. I ignore her and move forward. That's stupid; I don't care what she says. All I know is that I'm here to get my visa. I push through the crowd as if I'm swimming in a stormy ocean, dragging my suitcase behind me and elbowing the people who come in my way.

I can finally clearly see the top of the building behind tall, metal gates, the top of the revolutionary guards' heads, and the tips of their guns raised toward the sky. This is all that is visible above the crowd. I stand on the tip of my toes and poke my head up to see. My suitcase tumbles and gets caught in between people's legs. Letting go of Big Brown would be like letting a trusted friend slip away from my hands. I hold on tight. "I'm sorry, Big Brown," I whisper as I look down at her. I feel selfish. I wish all these people would disappear and let me do what I came here for.

The beautiful, wide-stretched, red-brick building is now minutes from where I stand. Tall, stone pillars stand majestically on either side of the entrance. I've never seen such a huge building. I can only see part of a long, winding driveway that I imagine leads to pathways that wind through breathtaking gardens. Green grass covers the grounds here, and tall trees spread their branches toward the sky. The desert climate of my home city, Shiraz, does not offer such a lush view. My dream of living in the US is about to come true. My heart is beating hard in my chest. I feel ten pounds lighter, like I am about to fly. All I must do is go through those gates, enter the embassy, and ask them to stamp my passport with a US student visa. I'm only a few meters away, making direct eye contact with my freedom.

As I get closer, I notice the portable fences erected as a barrier surrounding and imprisoning the embassy compound. Revolutionary guards are patrolling behind the barrier. The guards all look alike with matching army clothing. They have bushy beards and mustaches. They look terrifying. I didn't make eye contact with them. My mother always said your eyes are windows to your soul, and from the look of their empty and emotionless eyes, I don't feel like getting familiar with their souls.

I want to call and get their attention, but their rage as they yell at people to move away from the fence area stops me. A few guards pass by, but I don't have the guts to call upon them.

A guard passes by near the fence where I'm standing, but he ignores my pleas for help and walks away as if no one seems to care how important it is to get my passport stamped. My body heats up. As a guard walks by again, I raise my arms and bang my fist hard on the fence to get his attention. A shooting pain goes down my hand and travels to my arm. The bastard doesn't even turn to look at me. I hold my arm in pain, letting go of Big Brown. Quickly, I grab her handle again, which calms my nerves.

I lean over to the portable fence, letting go of Big Brown's handle. A revolutionary guard who looks like he has an agenda walks by close enough. I grab onto his khaki jacket. He has a deadly and intimidating expression on his face. His furrowed, bushy eyebrows send a chill down my body. Touching men has been forbidden since the revolution, but I have no choice. This is my only chance to reach my dream. I find the courage to hang on to him. A shiver goes down my spine as I glance at his machine gun.

"Sir, sir! I need to go inside the embassy!" I hold my passport and university admission up in front of him with the other hand, but he's busy keeping the crowd away. "Please! I need to go inside the embassy! Look!"

"*Na!*" he yells at me. "We got hostages in there."

"But I've got a university admission!" I yell again, pushing my university admission slip into his face. He swiftly detaches himself and, pushing his gun against my chest, uses it to shove me away. It feels like the tip of his gun has cut through my sternum. I bend forward in excruciating pain, but, undeterred, I rise again.

"What does that mean?" I ask. I feel like a child learning a new word.

"We've got them all as hostages in the devil's house; no one can go inside. Understand?" His voice is deep, filled with venom. I understand what hostage means now. My jaw drops wide open as I finally understand that the Americans in the building are being kept there against their will. They are captives.

I can't imagine how someone could capture someone. It is scary. I am shaking from fear and fuming with anger at the same time, because not only did I learn about the hostage crisis this way, but also the chances of getting my visa stamped were close to nothing.

The crowd around me is still chanting, "Down with the USA!" I linger around for a couple of hours, hoping in vain that something might change, but the crowd is getting thicker and thicker. My dream of freedom has washed away before my very eyes.

Tears pour down my face as I realize my future looks bleak and my only chance to escape the regressive nation has been sabotaged. My eyes reflect the despair as my remaining will is crushed.

I back away in sheer distress. A sense of numbness settles in as I stare back at the tall, metal gates surrounding the US Embassy. These gates now represent the demise of my hopes for freedom. I feel stuck, like a captive, wrists bound with handcuffs, feeling no less than a hostage.

Brave Little Girl

Fearlessness is not only possible, it is the ultimate
joy. When you touch nonfear, you are free.
—Thích Nhất Hạnh

My mother was raised in a middle-class family that was well-respected in the Esfahani neighborhood for being trustworthy and pious Shia Muslims. Esfahan, the capital of Iran during the Safavid dynasty, had long been a fundamental religious city in Iran.

When my mother was a little girl, Reza Shah Pahlavi, the first king of the Pahlavi dynasty, decided to liberate the nation's women with his progressive policies. He ordered women to remove their *chadors* (head coverings). In a religious city like Esfahan, these new policies were heretical.

I was shocked to hear how different times were back then as opposed to now. Women were forced to remove their coverings even when they didn't want to. My mother was one of them. She explained in her terms how bizarre it felt to roam around without a *chador* wrapped around her.

"Were the rules always as strict as they are now?" I asked her one night. I remember that conversation vividly because her body language changed completely when I asked her that question. Her bright eyes suddenly looked devoid of pleasure and joy, with sadness taking over her features.

"Rules are always strict for women, my child," she said that night. She didn't dwell on it any further, nor did I pester her, but from that limited interaction, I knew what she was trying to convey. Bodily autonomy was not accessible to women in any era. My mother suffered the traumas of it, and it is now my sisters' and my turn to bear the bruises. Ironically, under the shah's father, the ones who wanted to cover were punished as an incentive for them to remove their coverings, while now, the ones who did not wish to cover were lashed, so it is always sad to be a woman.

"Reza Shah, the first king of the Pahlavi dynasty's regime, didn't grant us freedom. We were still confined in various ways," my mother said.

"Oppression can have different faces, Mother," I remember whispering back to her.

From time to time, she would try to describe how life was when she was little. Freedom to choose was not authorized for women. She described how she felt when stripped of such an integral part of her attire and identity.

"No woman was to go out with a *chador*. It was like being naked. We would rather stay home for as long as it takes than go out unveiled."

My mother has always covered herself, and that's how I know she represented herself. She was not a very chatty woman to begin with, but when emotions struck her, she would often start a conversation. She would share snippets from her childhood. One summer afternoon, she told me more about the regime she was raised under and how women were treated then.

"When I was a little girl, Parvin, your grandmother took me and all your aunts to the *Hammam* (women's public bath). We would leave home long before dawn, tiptoeing through the alleys in the dark to get to the *Hammam*. Children had to be quiet so the government authorities wouldn't catch us in our *chadors*. Removing the *chador* was horrifying for us. It is a sin to show your body and hair to men. So, your grandmother would do anything to avoid that for us. It was a tough time, those days, for women.

"'Keep walking and look down' is what your grandmother would tell me and your aunts as we walked back home from the *Hammam*.

"'Don't take such big steps. Stick to my side and do not chatter.' She feared our big steps would attract attention. 'Why are they looking at us like that?' my sister, your aunt, asked Mother about the leering stares we would receive from random men, and you know what she said, Parvin? 'They always do.'"

At that moment, witnessing my mother speak so openly about her experiences left me without words. I was completely absorbed by her tales and the challenges she faced as a child. Not once did I interject as she began recounting her past.

"Whenever we would go out, it felt like an adventure. Your grandmother wanted us to cover ourselves, but the government would take strict action if they saw a child covering their heads. It's a strange world we live in."

I witnessed a new kind of despair in her eyes as she said that; it contrasted with the smile lines etched on her face. The way she would recall her past always gave me goosebumps because, through her voice alone, I could tell how a big chunk of her childhood was plucked from her hands. I would often ask Mom about her childhood. It was obvious, from how she changed the subject or tried to busy herself each time, that she was uncomfortable talking about some of her past experiences.

Some memories were too difficult to relive. A couple of months after the revolution, she started talking more about her first marriage and the things she had to go through. Mom was sitting in the living room, warming up by the little heating stove in the middle of the room.

It was cold outside. The sun shone through the stained-glass window, reflecting onto the living room walls and rugs, making the room extraordinarily colorful. Mom was knitting something; I don't quite remember what it was. I sat beside her on the blanket when she decided to open up. I still remember her blank expression masking utmost suffering. Her dejected eyes focused on the needle and the woven material as she started talking.

"My father, your grandfather, was a well-respected elder for being a trustworthy, pious Shia Muslim in Esfahan. People traveled from far away just to hear his opinion, resolving the issues they were facing. Our family was not rich but middle-class, well-known, and well-respected, all because my father was a very good man."

She beamed with immense pride as she brought up her father. Then she leaned back as she continued.

"Reza Shah Pahlavi decided to liberate the nation's women with his progressive policies, but we were not ready for that. He ordered women to remove their head coverings. *Chador* was like a security blanket for us women. Taking it away felt like ripping off a limb for us. We had been wearing *chadors* for generations. It was part of being a woman in those days.

It was horrifying when the police caught women wearing them and forced them to be bareheaded. That is how we all lived in fear at the time. You don't understand how hard it was for us to hide at home and not be able to go out. I wish my mother were alive to see this day when women are forced to put on their *hijab* again.

I was a very active child, almost as daring as the boys my age. Often, when I was forbidden to do something or knew I was in trouble, I climbed the old mulberry tree in your grandparents' yard to hide away. Your grandmother would call me, but I would just sit up in the tree quietly so she couldn't find me. Those were some of the best days of my life."

A tiny smile appeared on her lips, and she became more vibrant as she talked about her childhood.

"The boys of the family would make fun of me because I was nutty and rebellious and climbed trees like a boy. Girls were not allowed to do lots of things, like learn to read or write *Farsi*. It was deemed unnecessary for us. We all knew our future would lie in taking care of households and raising children. So, I never went to a regular school to learn *Farsi*.

"I think I was five years old when a neighbor taught me to read the Qur'an in Arabic. Of course, I never understood the meaning of what I was reading, but I still had to learn all the scripts. My teacher would say, 'The Qur'an is the book of God. Every Muslim ought to know how to read it.'

"The neighbor's teaching wasn't for free, you know. In return for learning the Qur'an, I weaved Persian rugs for her, which she sold for a profit. At the age of five, my hands were tiny, and I could not make the knots properly. With every mistake I made, she would hit me on the hands with a piece of tree branch. The pain made me work harder to not make mistakes. This is how I learned to weave the beautiful rugs you see that people buy to cover their floors.

"All your aunts learned to read the Qur'an, as I did, but learning to read and write *Farsi* was a privilege that was only reserved for boys. So, all your uncles were sent to school to learn *Farsi* while your aunts and I could only learn to read the Qur'an."

Then she let out a big sigh and continued, again proudly referring to my father.

"Your father was a good man when he encouraged me to attend adult school in my late thirties so that I could learn how to read and write *Farsi*. It was a life-altering step for me. It was a long time ago, but I feel embarrassed to talk about some of my past. In olden times, people were really barbaric toward their girls. It was unfair and unjust how they treated them, but it was a societal norm."

When I asked my mother about her first marriage, I could see her face flushing and her eyes gazing at the patterns of the Persian rug we were sitting on. Her energy visibly changed. She looked shy and embarrassed. I knew she didn't like to remember she was once married to anyone other than my father. With a look of child-like innocence in her eyes, she responded.

"Oh, it was a long time ago. People didn't know as much as they know now." I felt like she was trying to defend her parents or perhaps make the conversation short.

"Girls were a burden to the family. It was a custom for our families to give away their daughters at the early age of eight or nine. We didn't have a say in it as girls, you see. A daughter should be a virgin when she gets married, and teenage girls are too hard for parents to handle or police. Families didn't want to risk a girl losing her virginity and bringing shame to the family. Sometimes, unmarried pregnant girls would be killed by their own families, even if they were raped. To avoid this tragedy, a family would give prepubescent daughters away in marriage. This way, the husband's family could raise and mold the girl to their expectations.

"Boys had it all; they always do. They could live with their families after marriage. They could raise their own family and take care of their elderly parents at the same time. That was how the in-laws would mold the child bride to the way that best suited their family.

"It makes me feel empty inside when I think about the past. It is hard to talk about the vulnerability I felt back then and still do, even now that many decades have passed."

She continued, and with each word, the weight in her chest seemed to lift, gradually easing the burden as she spoke.

"I was given away to a fifty-year-old man to be wed when I was eight. Your grandfather had a friend at the bazaar where he worked who had just lost his wife and was looking for a new one. My father offered him one of his daughters, and that daughter was me."

My eyes widened as Mom said this. I held my breath, utterly disturbed. I covered my mouth with my hands, determined not to disrupt her as she continued her gut-wrenching tale.

"I met him for the very first time at our wedding ceremony. I was initially delighted by the festive celebrations and music of the wedding and the fact that I was receiving so many fancy new clothes. I had so much attention from my family and friends that I felt like a princess from a storybook."

She shook her head, reminiscing about the child-like innocence she possessed on that fateful day—because she was merely a child after all. Then, with poignant reflection, she resumed recalling her memories from her first wedding.

"By the end of the evening, I was terrified and confused. My husband's family had to physically force me to leave with them, pulling me away by my hands. Up until that moment, my little mind could not put two and two together to realize marriage meant I had to leave my family and the home I grew up in.

"I pleaded, begged, and cried a flood of tears, wanting to stay with my parents, but no one listened. As if I had no voice, I screamed silently. I felt betrayed. My parents didn't want me anymore. I was too young to understand the rigid traditions of my culture. All I wanted was to stay with my family. They watched me cry and beg but let me get taken away."

Mom took a deep breath, let out a loud sigh, and then she continued.

"It was acceptable for the little girl to cry when she was taken away from her family, but once the daughter is gone, she is no longer her parent's problem or responsibility. *What did I do wrong? Why don't my parents want me anymore?* I thought. *Maybe if I hadn't climbed that mulberry tree, my parents would have kept me.* I thought I must have done something wrong for them to give me away.

"I was traumatized by the thought of sleeping with this strange old man on the wedding night. It wasn't something comprehensible for an eight-year-old child bride. Until the night before the wedding, I had slept in my own bed in a room shared with my four sisters, but that night, it was to be different. I was only eight! I had been playing with the dolls my mother made me until the day before, and now I had to sleep with an old man. It was such a jarring and disturbing change in my life situation, and I didn't know how to cope with it. My head feels like exploding when those memories resurrect in my mind."

A flush of red tinted Mom's face as she attempted to conceal the tears welling up in her eyes. She averted her gaze downward, feigning interest in the intricate patterns of the rug beneath us. Eventually, a few minutes later, she gathered the courage to become brutally direct with me.

"Yes, I was raped repeatedly most every night."

Mom paused to watch the shattering effect this declaration had on me. Then, she resumed her confessions.

"All I wanted was to go back home, but Esfahan was a big city, and I was too young to be able to find my parents' home by myself. I cried and begged the old man to take me to my parents, but of course, he wouldn't listen to me; I was just a child bride, and he owned me.

"God bless my parents' souls. They never visited me. They thought that seeing their faces would make me homesick and that they would be forced to take me back home. I would hide in the closet with my knees to my chest, weeping, mourning, and praying for my family to come to rescue me. It was the only place I felt safe.

"After constantly pleading for months to go back home, I finally gave up and accepted that I would never see my family again. I started believing that I was not wanted. I did not know I was in deep depression, but I remember wishing I was dead.

"After a year of being in captivity, one summer day, when I felt no one was around, I slowly walked out of the closet into the yard. There were no adults around. It was a hot day. I sat under the maple tree, finally feeling a semblance of freedom away from the closet. I noticed the old man's little grandchildren playing in the yard. They were around the same age as me, and they reminded me of my beloved siblings, whom I missed dearly. I held my tears back, so the children didn't see me crying. I didn't want them to make fun of me.

"As I was sitting under the tree watching them, one of the children approached me and asked, 'Would you like to play with us?' I looked around to make sure she was talking to me.

"For the first time in months, I could feel a little spark of joy bubble up inside me. A smile broke out across my frozen face. I shyly accepted the offer and went to join them. I became a child once again and played hide-and-seek all day without a care in the world.

"The day flew by quickly, and before I knew it, it was afternoon, and my old-man husband came home. He walked into the yard and grew furious when he saw me playing with his grandchildren. 'How dare you play with children? You are not a child. You are my wife. You should act like one!' he shouted, and he violently beat me with his leather belt.

"I don't know if God will ever forgive him. My entire body was bruised and oozing blood from welts in exposed areas. 'Please stop; I won't do it again. Please, please, I beg you,' I pledged."

Mom's lower lip and chin began to quiver, resembling a young girl desperately trying to stifle her tears. It was painful to watch her in that state, but she was determined to continue.

"After a while, he finally got tired and stopped the beating. Sobbing, I went back to hide in the closet again, but, you know, playing with those children was the only way I could escape being depressed and homesick for a few hours. The days would pass quickly when I was spending time with them. Memories of playing with my siblings would come alive, and I would pretend I was playing with them again.

"So, when no adult was home, I would sneak outside and play with the children. Don't get me wrong; I would get into trouble and receive a beating every single time, but to me, it was worth it. Spending time with those children kept me alive. It was a matter of surviving, I guess, even if it meant getting beaten by the adults in the house.

"Those kids were God-sent. I think it was a couple of years that I endured captivity by the old man. During these long years, I had no contact with the outside world at all, including my own family.

"Finally, I was allowed to visit my family. I was over the moon, looking forward to reuniting with my siblings and parents. When I arrived at my parent's home, I knelt and kissed the ground. This was where I was raised and had lived all of my childhood memories. Ever since I was dragged away to be the old man's property, I dreamed of this day when I would finally return home. The entire day felt like a fairytale to me, when the princess who had been kept prisoner by a monster finally freed herself.

"Well, the evening arrived, and before I knew it, it was time for me to go back to the old man's home. He was waiting impatiently by the door to take me away, but I refused. Nothing and no one could convince me to leave with him. I stood my ground and begged and cried my eyes out for my parents not to send me back. It was so devastating for my parents to see me this way that they were convinced to keep me, at least for that night."

Even at a tender age, Mom's pride shone through, evident in her expression. She reveled in the memory of standing up for herself and showcasing an extraordinary amount of strength as she continued talking about her childhood.

"After that, no matter how much your grandparents tried to convince me to go back, I refused and protested. Finally, my parents had no choice but to ask the old man to divorce me. My father realized that I had been abused. The old man did not accept that, arguing that his wife was his property and that I must do as he said. He tried to threaten your grandparents, but since they couldn't convince me to go back, they refused to send me back. He even tried to buy my affection by sending me all kinds of gifts, but I still wouldn't budge.

"I wasn't always like this, weak and tired. I was a rebellious girl. It was tough, and I finally found my way back to my parents' house. You know, your aunts were all given away at a young age, too, but they all obeyed and accepted the life that was laid out for them.

"The entire neighborhood was talking about my divorce, but the only important thing for me was being free at home with my family. The freedom I felt after being in captivity for so long was indescribable. It was as if I had two wings and was flying."

My mother's story horrified me. The belief in our culture was that girls must be married off as soon as possible. That was part of the tradition in most families, including mine. Even though my mother had gone through a terrible time as a child bride, the tradition continued from one generation to the next. By the time my older sisters were fourteen or fifteen, they were forced to marry the men arranged for them. As the last unmarried daughter at age eighteen, the pressure on me to get married came from all directions. I was intensely terrified of the idea of continuing the patterns imposed on my sisters.

For me, embracing the idea of a forced marriage felt like the demise of all my hopes and aspirations. Nonetheless, there were moments when I couldn't shake the sense of inadequacy compared to the other girls who were already wed. The life around me brought me to the realization that I must take action in my life since marriage was not a viable choice for me.

3

Revolution

For most of history, anonymous was a woman.
—VIRGINIA WOOLF

After my dad's death, everything changed.

The flowers ceased to blossom on the street, newfound despair consumed the neighborhood, the winds veered away, and my home remained untouched by the joyful breeze that once embraced those walls. The situation inside the house was much more drastic. The silent weight of melancholy lingered in every nook and cranny of the house.

There were days when I would witness pin-drop silence.

I struggled to get my life together again after *Bābā's* passing. All he left me was a mountain of grief that suffocated me on lonely nights. My sisters wept constantly when they would visit, but no amount of mourning came closer to the state of my mother. Her profound silence was loud enough to pierce the very fabric of our souls. She stopped smiling after that. She barely took a moment for herself and immersed herself in household chores, which I was sure she sought as a coping mechanism so she wouldn't have to mourn Dad.

My mother devoted most of her hours to the kitchen, preparing delightful meals. I knew she cherished prepping food for me and my siblings, but only

I could tell from the upside-down frown on her face that she was harboring a tremendous amount of anguish. After some time, my sisters' casual visits to the house manifested into a ritual of sorts where they would see us every Friday for a healthy feast prepared by Mom. My mother and I would drown ourselves in kitchen duties to provide a bountiful weekend for my sisters. My mother always looked forward to spending a wholesome time together as a family. All three of my sisters would arrive before noon with their respective families and spend the entire day.

I remember one specific gathering clearly; it was a bright, sunny day. The powerful, nutty aroma of fresh basmati rice traveled to my nose when I woke up. My mother's meals were no less than a labor. I would often find her doing half the preparation late into the night before. I entered the kitchen, and there she was, her hands dipped in marinated chicken she'd prepared the day before, deliciously submerged in a concoction of homemade yogurt and saffron with various spices. Her fingers were lathered in yogurt, and the bowl of soaked rice rested on the kitchen counter.

"Where have you been? Now go, hurry up. Make sure the living room is clean and your brothers-in-law's pajamas are ready," she instructed me. I understood why she would let the homely duties engulf her entire being, keeping her on her toes. She would always be seen in a frantic state when my sisters would visit, panicking about everything. She needed something occupying her mind so she wouldn't have to come face-to-face with Dad's absence, and I knew her memories of him tormented her too.

"So many dishes get dirty when you prepare one of these meals," she said while washing the extra pots and pans after she finished the chicken.

"*Māmān*, pajamas are ready, and the living room is clean. Anything else I should be doing?" I assured her and asked her about other chores I could help her out with, hoping my involvement would bring a smile to her face.

"Good. Make sure the yard is clean, and remember to turn the water on in the pond for the children to play."

"OK, *Māmān*."

As my sisters arrived one by one, accompanied by their families, the house was filled with lively chaos that rekindled the warmth of our shared memories. Laughter echoed as my nieces and nephews ran around, infusing the space with their mischief. I adored my nieces and nephews when, in the midst of this beautiful day, they would eagerly rush toward their grandma and me, enveloping us in tight hugs and savoring the moment. Each one was a little fireball of enthusiasm.

"*Khale* [Auntie] Parvin, can you play with us in the yard?" they each hollered one by one.

"Of course. Why don't you guys carry on? I will join you in a second," I yelled back.

Ellie, my oldest sister, entered the living room. "*Māmān*, I could smell your *Tahchin polo* all the way from the end of the street. So good," she said with a hunger evident in her eyes.

She's always been the foodie of the family. Mom's cheeks reddened at the compliment. The way her eyes would shine as one of us would applaud her food was priceless. I loved seeing her like that. This was probably the first time I had witnessed a small smile on her face after a long time. It was just for a second that her mouth curled up. I had thought I wouldn't be able to see her like that ever again.

"Of course, anything for my family," she had said. It was not what she said but the way she uttered those words with a deep exhale of pride and joy that was evident in her eyes. I knew she wasn't just talking about food.

One by one, the three men changed into their matching pajamas. They gathered on the blanket spread across the Persian rugs, leaning against the hand-embroidered cushions specially embroidered by Mom.

"We look like triplets with these pajamas," Ali said with a chuckle while he rested his hand on his round belly and relaxed back on the cushion behind him.

"Obviously, with different sets of parents," Maz replied as he stepped into the living room, crouching a bit to avoid hitting his head on the door frame.

"Come on, guys, let's drink the tea before it gets cold," Ronny, my third brother-in-law, interrupted as he added another blanket under himself to cushion his bony frame. The trio huddled together, indulging in lively conversations about politics and their individual professions, while they each sipped my mom's tea through a sugar cube betwen their front teeth. The slurping sound echoed through the living room.

On the other hand, my sisters were all gathered in the kitchen, catching up and chit-chatting while Mom skillfully prepared a delicious meal to serve.

"Ah, so nice to be at home, like the old days," one of my sisters said.

"For once, I don't have to worry about the children," another concurred, and they all vented. Kids can be a handful. Besides, as much as I love each one of them, they were pretty frightening as a bunch.

"You get tired of the demands of your husband and constant nagging of the kids."

"When you marry young, you miss out on living life. It's all about responsibilities from the moment you open your eyes."

Mom listened to my sister's complaints and then huffed, "You were much older than me when you married. I was only eight years old when they gave me away." Mom exhaled audibly and shook her head from side to side out of annoyance.

I felt relieved as I listened to my sisters complain about their husbands' constant nagging and the motherly duties of catering to their children twenty-four seven. While I had my own set of challenges, I couldn't help but feel grateful that I wasn't trapped in the fate of an early marriage like my mother and sisters. It might sound selfish, and while I sympathize with them, every time I reflect on their lives, mine doesn't seem as harsh.

As I entered the yard, I found the kids in their favorite spot—the fishpond. Watching them swim with the goldfish, feeling the ticklish sensations as the slippery, soft bodies brushed against their skin, brought back memories of my own childhood. I spent hours swimming with the fishes in the pond, shrieking with laughter. In those moments, Dad's voice would echo from his room, a distant but fond memory.

"I told you to be quiet. Now, you look at what you did. You made your father upset."

Mom would run to catch me. I reflect upon my chaotic childhood because I was also mischievous, like my nieces and nephews. Mom's voice brought me back to the kids having fun at the pond.

"Get out of the pond. You will catch a cold," Mom yelled over the children's laughter.

The way she shouted so gleefully made me feel warm that day. The kids sprayed Mom with water from the garden hoses, prompting her to run inside, laughter echoing in the air. The sparkle in her eyes revealed a profound joy and contentment, which was a rare commodity in those days.

As noon approached, we gathered around for lunch. A vibrant *Sofreh* tablecloth adorned the carpeted living room floor. I set all the plates, spoons, and forks down neatly. The spread included a large serving plate of *Tahchin polo*, a generous bowl of salad, and another dish featuring cucumber salad with yogurt—a Persian specialty.

We all sat down around the tablecloth and had lunch in peace. That day was one of the most serene days of my life. Especially after Dad's passing, we needed a joyful moment of togetherness filled with shared memories that kept us warm, and Mom's delicious food was the centerpiece of the gathering. If Dad were here, he would lighten the day even more with his loving sensitivity and laughter echoing the walls.

"God bless your father's soul, Parvin. Turn on your *Bābā*'s old radio. Let's see what they say today," Ali said in the middle of lunch.

"Ya, I heard about the *mullah* in Iraq. Have you heard about him? Let's see what the news says," Ronny chimed in on the conversation.

I quickly got up to carefully turn on Dad's radio, ensuring the knob stayed in place. The news was all about a man called Ayatollah Khomeini, who had been exiled for many years. He was apparently coming back to overthrow the shah and free Iran.

"What?" one of my brothers-in-law said.

"Who is Ayatollah? I never heard of him," Mom asked, and I had the same question in my mind. No one seemed to know the man. We listened to the radio for a while. Maybe one of my brothers-in-law would enlighten us about this *mullah* they had been discussing. They loved talking about politics and news like my father.

The announcer reported, "Breaking news: Ayatollah Khomeini, currently in exile, says he's stepping up to lead the country, aiming to create a better Iran for its people."

We all shared a collective wounded look when we heard the announcement. "Just like that? How can he do such a thing? He can't overthrow the shah and his government. He is too powerful for anyone to overthrow," Ali expressed his disbelief.

"It is probably all fake news," Ronny said.

"*Na*, it is impossible. Shah is too powerful for anyone to dare getting close to him," Maz said.

The entire afternoon was consumed by discussions about this Ayatollah and the shah, accompanied by tea and my mom's homemade cookies. The news was a shock to everyone, including me. The concept of an exiled

Ayatollah and his mission was new to me. I remained baffled throughout that gathering, with a conflicted feeling brewing within me.

Even Mrs. Karim, our next-door neighbor and a usually reserved religious woman who didn't follow the news closely, showed keen interest in understanding the unfolding events. It was a break from our routine when she'd occasionally join us for a cup of tea in the afternoons. Her presence would always lift my mom's mood and spirits.

One of those days when our doorbell rang incessantly, I could tell from the rhythmic pattern of the bell that it was her.

"That must be Mrs. Karim. She is the only one who rings the doorbell like this."

"Go open the door for her," Mom instructed me, so I ran to the yard and opened the big, yellow, double-iron door.

"Come in, Mrs. Karim. *Māmān* is inside."

"God bless you, girl. I won't stay long. I brought some *sholleh zard*, rice pudding for you and your mom."

I was pleased to see her. Aside from mom's cooking, Mrs. Karim's food always brought a big smile to my face. This time, she retrieved a bowl of beautifully presented saffron rice pudding decorated with cinnamon, almonds, and pistachio from under her black *chador*.

"Here, take it inside for your mother."

"Thank you, Mrs. Karim. Come inside, please. My mom is waiting for you."

"*Ghabeli nadareh azizam*" [Oh, it is nothing, dear].

She smiled coyly at me before removing her shoes and entering the hallway to our living room. I walked behind her to show my respect to an elder.

Mom broke into a big, beaming smile when she saw her. "*Salam* [Hello], Mrs. Karim. So lovely to see you."

They kissed three times on the cheeks and hugged.

"It is so hot outside." Then she removed her *chador* scarf, exposing her beautiful, long, braided hair, and rolled her sleeves up before settling on a blanket on the floor.

"Parvin, go fetch the tea from the kitchen," Mom said.

I hurried away toward the Samovar teapot set in the kitchen.

"Mrs. Karim, would you like a sugar cube with your tea, or dates?"

"*Zahmat nakesh* [Don't worry, dear]. I will have my tea with rice pudding."

I came back with a tray holding three cups of tea. Mrs. Karim rested her right elbow on her knee, supporting her chin with her palm. Her eyebrows furrowed, and her mouth drooped in deep thought.

"You know, this Ayatollah Khomeini who says he wants to come back to the country? He wears Prophet Mohammad's traditional attire and turban. He speaks the words of God. He must be right," Mrs. Karim said.

"You think he won't do anything wrong?" Mom said, scratching her head with concern. I listened to their back-and-forth chatter.

This traditional religious attire wasn't worn by many but just a few people in Iran. One can compare it with clerical clothing priests wear in churches. The attire came with trust and respect among Muslims, including Mrs. Karim. Something about the whole ordeal about this *mullah* rubbed me wrong. I found myself getting lost in the ocean of uncertainty and fear.

After Dad passed away, the tradition of listening to BBC News was carried on by Mom and me. So, one day, BBC broadcasted Khomeini's messages.

"Shah is a criminal. I will slap him in the mouth. He is stealing people's oil money. Such a rich country should have free utilities. Everyone should be treated equally."

His messages were straightforward and clear for people to protest against the shah. Each of his speeches motivated his people to rise and participate in riots against the shah. He instilled hatred for the shah among the masses through his frequent speeches.

Hearing his speeches unlocked new terror within me. I still remember one particular night. It was past midnight. I was startled from a deep sleep; I sat upright at the echo of distant shouting outside the house. My heart started fluttering in my chest as I sat on the edge of my bed, straining to decipher the unclear words. I sprinted to check on my mother, who was already up, peering through the window.

"What is happening, *Māmān*? What is with all the noise?" I asked as I clutched her *chador* in my hands.

"I'm not sure. I think some people are on the rooftops," she replied, uncertain and scared herself.

Her expression turned anxious as the noises ceased to be distant. I sensed they originated from somewhere nearby in the neighborhood. Too frightened to venture into the yard myself, my mom decided to open the window and witness the chaos firsthand.

"Can you hear what they are saying?" she asked me with an innocent expression on her face.

"I think they are saying *Marg bar shah* [death to Shah], *Khomeini rahbar* [Khomeini is our leader]," I replied.

Although I couldn't hear it too clearly either from all the chaos and loud shouting, I could comprehend some phrases since the people on the rooftops were pretty close.

"God will not forgive people who scare people in the middle of the night like this," Mom said, letting out a loud sigh. That night was just the beginning of the messy state of affairs. After that night, this uproar started to bleed into our daily lives. Every now and then since that night, a group of people would rise and protest on the streets against the shah. They would have slogans and banners in hand with aggressive chants upon their lips.

"Shah must leave."

"Khomeini is our leader."

"Down with Shah."

Hearing those vicious, loud chants took me back to when I was in elementary school. Every time Shah would visit Shiraz and pass by my school, my school would arrange a session outside where we, as students, were instructed to line up on the side of the street, waving a little Iranian flag with the following chants in favor of the shah.

"Long live Shah."

"Long live the queen."

The scene would unfold before us when Shah and his wife, Queen Farah, waved at us from their convertible car. Those days remain vivid in my memory, as I would eagerly stand on my tiptoes, waving my flag as high as I could to catch their attention. Their presence had a remarkable impact on the masses, especially on schools and educational institutes. Their visits became sacred and became the hot topic of discussion in Shiraz. People would talk about the shah and his wife like gossip mongers looking for fresh intel. They talked about the king and queen's larger-than-life appeal, their lifestyle, their wardrobe—anything and everything.

"I know what I want to be when I grow up. I will marry the Prince Reza and become a princess." I remember being so moved by Shah and his wife's charming aura that I dreamed about such things. I would desire the life that Shah presented to us at that time, and I wasn't the only one.

"No, I want to marry him," one of my friends from school would reply, sending each of us into fits of laughter after the procession would end.

My fantasy world, with its crystal castle, shattered around me, swallowed by quicksand. Shah, who became a comforting figure like a father during my childhood, had subconsciously replaced my actual father—a strong protector who would always be there. As the nation's army attempted to force protesters off the streets, students quickly retaliated with handmade Molotov cocktails and anti-Shah graffiti sprayed across the city walls.

I wanted to shake these people and remind them. I wanted to rattle them to their core and get them to recall all the positive contributions and dutiful favors he had bestowed upon the country, but everyone seemed to forget about his benevolence.

"Wake up. Don't you remember how important Shah was for us?"

During the last year of high school and after I finished, these rampant protests became a part of our lives.

Within a short span of time, Shiraz, famously known as the city of flowers and poetry, the birthplace of great poets Hafiz and Sadi, fell from grace. The people were devastated to witness the gradual demise of the city's essence. The statues of the shah, dignifying the heart of the town as monuments commemorating his power, were cast down in defiance by Khomeini's supporters. The ancient fort, a testament to the Zandi dynasty's history, stood neglected, adorned with bullet holes, whispering tales of ancient glory.

Amid all the destruction, the familiar echoes of gunshots resonated like distant popcorn popping and ominous explosions nearby. A wave of terror agonized each street of Shiraz. Each shot carried a haunting melody, starkly contrasting the city's poetic heritage. In the refuge of our home, my mother and I sought solace in the furthest bathroom, creating a cocoon of safety. As we covered our ears and closed our eyes, I clung to my mom's black *chador* as she hid me in her arms. Like an ongoing whisper on our tongue, a silent prayer concealed our presence like a secret.

"You can come out now. It is over." My mother checked by peeking through the window.

"Are you sure, *Māmān*?" I asked, still hesitant to leave the cocoon of safety.

"This is insane. What if one of these gunshots kills somebody? What if it kills a child?" my mother said in utter distress.

Incidents like these didn't cease anytime soon. There were plenty of times when I would find myself hidden in one corner of the bathroom, shaking in fear as gunshots would pierce the winds of Shiraz.

In times like those, I truly felt like I was a part of one of those wild Western movies I used to watch on the weekends on our tiny, black-and-white television—the ones full of mayhem but, in this situation, with an Eastern touch.

Six years after my father's death, financial restrictions started suffocating us. My mother struggled to make ends meet and provide. We limited our budget, making sure nothing was wasted. We feared our rations declining.

"*Enshallah*, when Ayatollah comes to Iran, we don't have to pay for utilities and medical care. Life will be easier for us. We won't have to struggle anymore," Mom said one day.

I knew she was hopeful that maybe he would change the course of history by bringing prosperity, especially by fulfilling the desires of middle-class and poor people, but I was still suspicious of him. The way he talked about people in rage, the way he held himself, and the way he spent most of his words in his speeches to spread enmity amongst the people of Iran made me uneasy.

"What is wrong with Shah?" I asked my mother, with a hint of resentment toward the new uproar.

"Shah's father wasn't a good man forcing us to remove our *hijab*. Those days were tough on me and your grandmother. Finally, someone is going to bring back the *hijab*. That's a good thing, *dokhtaram* [my daughter]," she said as she kissed my forehead.

Frequently, I made the mistake of presenting my desire to never observe *hijab*. "Mom, but I don't like *hijab*. Women shouldn't be forced to wear if they don't want to." This would create an air of disagreement between us. I often found myself in a hard place where I would engage in heated arguments. I even tried to explain to her one time how I am not opposed to *hijab* but that I believe in the freedom to choose what people, especially women, want to do with their lives and their bodies, and this would receive brutal backlash from her. Soon, I came to the swift conclusion that neither of us would change our minds, so it was better to let it be, but I felt misunderstood in my own house. It felt like I was traveling between two dimensions and not knowing which side I belonged to. I was neither here nor there.

Every altercation between my mother and me deepened this sense of loss, as if my freedom was like sand slipping away through my fingers. *Where am I going from here? What am I supposed to do when my mother doesn't understand the root of the problem?* With thoughts like these, my future looked bleak, my hopes and dreams crumbling before my eyes.

While all this was happening, I was mourning the loss of what I had— mourning my investment as a child with both Shah and Queen Farah. Queen Farah's kind and angelic expressions and the wave of her hand on television were swiftly replaced by marches, crude noises, and loud, aggressive chants against the monarchy. The departure of the shah from Iran felt akin to losing my father once more. In just a few months, he and his family departed, and I watched as the 2,500-year-old kingdom, which had always filled me with pride, crumbled. The downfall of my country, something I never fathomed in my wildest dreams, shattered the illusion of living in a big, shiny bubble, abruptly dropping me back into the harsh embrace of reality.

The very people who used to chant "Long live Shah" when he used to visit Shiraz with his family, wave at him, and hold the flag with the lion, sword, and sun icon in the middle, were now chanting "Down with Shah" and "Shah must leave." It was difficult to witness all the glory and the magnificence of the shah dynasty ablaze and pro-Khomeini people feasting on the ashes of their kingdom.

A year-long mayhem finally succumbed to a definitive end on February 10, 1979, when Ayatollah Khomeini rose to power. Many of Shah's cabinet members escaped right after Shah's departure, while those who remained were captured. It all unfolded so quickly that I had no time to grapple with the situation sufficiently. All I wanted to do was escape this regressive horror. Every day, I would wake up to a new dystopia. The new regime used fear to control the populace by having newspapers start printing horrifying pictures of tortured and executed bodies of the captured shah's cabinet members.

Seeing those gruesome pictures on the back of newspapers churned my stomach uncomfortably every time.

Television and radio stations stopped playing music and movies or shows with women in them. Even the voices of women on the radio were blocked out. Women's involvement in any media was banned. It felt like women just vanished from the entertainment industry. Even female news reporters or journalists were forced to wear the *hijab* if they wanted to stay employed. The only sound you could hear from the radio station was the sound of the regime officials relaying the news, military music, or the reciting of Qur'an verses. People grew fearful, realizing what this new regime could do.

The stark difference between Shah and Khomeini's government was hard to digest as a woman living in Iran. I felt suffocated and invisible. Women were forced to comply with every demand if they wanted to keep their jobs.

Following this, the revolutionary guards spread themselves throughout every nook and cranny of the streets, becoming vigilant enforcers of compliance. Their watchful eyes bore down on everyone, ensuring strict adherence to their imposed laws. Women felt the weight of this surveillance, compelled to cover themselves in a veil of modesty in big, black *chadors*.

Slowly but surely, they found their status relegated to that of second-class citizens. The entire nation transformed into a colossal confinement, and I sensed my voice and dreams slipping away within this oppressive regime. I felt there was no way out of this.

Paving the Path

As you start to walk the way, the way appears.
— R U M I

When the revolution occurred, schools were temporarily shut down for an entire year due to the relentless protests and riots that grappled the nation. The daily demonstrations created an environment where even the most fundamental aspects of life became a challenge for working-class citizens.

The influence of Khomeini on the masses reached far beyond the realm of education. It cast a heavy shadow over schooling and all the bustling activities of shops, vendors, and merchants, disrupting the usual business flow. The once-vibrant markets were now quiet, with many establishments either closed or barely managing to survive amid the revolutionary chaos.

When I finally returned to school a year later, the echoes of the revolution were still reverberating through the streets. Getting back into the routine was tough for me. The recent upheaval had changed everything; I could feel those differences in every part of my daily life. It was a challenging adjustment. From the simple act of getting ready for school to the once-familiar routine of attending classes, everything bore the mark of Khomeini's influence and events unfolding during the preceding year.

The atmosphere was charged with uncertainty, and the disturbance caused by the revolution left an indelible impact on our educational environment. The first thing that caught me off guard when I returned to school was the sight of every girl in my school covered from head to toe in various dark-colored *hijabs*. It was perplexing, given that I attended an all-girls school. The peculiar aspect wasn't the veiling itself; it was unexpected because no men were in or around our classes, yet we were all entirely covered.

The impact of Khomeini's arrival had been anticipated, but no one foresaw the extent of the transformation. In the previous regime, under the shah, girls used to wear skirts in school. However, in Khomeini's government, not only were *hijabs* mandated, but even the covering of legs became a requirement, leading to the women being forbidden to wear skirts. The shift was so drastic, and the atmosphere in our school reflected the profound changes. Every woman working there was now veiled in a black *hijab*, symbolizing the adherence to the new rules.

One more thing I noticed upon returning to school was the striking absence of emotion and youthful antics. Everything felt so out of place and mundane, as if everyone wore a mask. The faces around me seemed laden with uncertainty and sadness. It became apparent that the silence and masked emotions stemmed from a collective apprehension about the current state of our country. The air was thick with unspoken tensions in my school. It was a time when even the slightest whisper could be misconstrued, and the weight of potential consequences stifled genuine expressions of belief or dissent.

Despite everything, I was still excited at the prospect of reuniting with friends after what felt like an eternity. The anticipation of engaging in long, meaningful chats and sharing food with them, as well as the laughter and gossip we shared in school, was the only source of joy.

The stark differences became instantly apparent as I entered the school on the first day. The once-girlish mingling atmosphere of my school now resounded with an unusual silence. It was something that had shifted in contrast to the previous lively and animated school days that I had remembered.

Despite my eagerness to rekindle friendships, the subdued atmosphere was hard to ignore—the brazen laughter during recess, the teasing, and the sheer drama—all gone. A new air of prohibition had enveloped our schools and the people of Iran.

Another discordant thing that caught my eye when we were all seated inside our classrooms was the absence of the framed pictures of Shah and Queen Farah that used to adorn the walls of our halls and classrooms. Every last one had been taken down, and the harsh reality set in—we were no longer students of Shah's regime. We had transformed into students in Khomeini's regime, and that realization weighed heavily on my heart.

I couldn't see any Iranian flags waving around. I wondered if they had been taken down too. Moreover, the morning ritual of reciting the national anthem before entering our respective classes was no longer given importance. I vividly recall a day when, sitting beside my friend, I inquired about the frenzy that seemed to unfold as I pointed to the vacant space on the wall where Shah's and Queen Farah's portraits once hung. Again, she shushed me, saying, "You can't talk about that. Don't speak of this to anyone else because the boys who discussed the shah were taken to jail or faced punishment."

The fear in my heart lingered, leaving a lasting impression of the consequences tied to even the slightest mention of Shah's regime. Throughout the rest of the school year, we had to tiptoe hesitantly.

I began to reminisce about the times before Khomeini took over, when girls would sing songs and dance to different rhythms in recess or during free time, especially when the teachers were absent. However, after a year, the entire landscape of our school had transformed. There were no more songs nor dancing around the classroom. The notion of women talking loudly, let alone dancing, seemed like a far-fetched and forbidden thought.

After the revolution, we finally graduated. One day, my friend Arie came to visit me and announced that she was getting married. I wasn't shocked to hear this news, but I was still moved. She informed me that she had a fiancé. I remember asking her about all the details and her plans for the future. I knew she wanted to marry early, but as a friend, I still wanted to see if she was doing this willingly and satisfied with her decision.

"Are you going to be happy?" I asked, genuinely curious, masking my sense of worry regarding her well-being.

"Of course, what other choice do we have?" she replied with a blank expression. She continued, disbelief evident in her eyes, like she had succumbed to her fate like all the other girls.

"At least, you know, I get to have my own life and family," she said with a tight smile plastered as if she were reassuring herself more than me. I sensed a mixture of anticipation and hope in her voice. She was one of my closest friends, so I pestered her more.

"But are you excited about it?" I asked, wanting to understand more about her feelings and the things she wanted.

She sensed what I was trying to do. Arie grabbed my hand and sighed. "It's not like I had a lot of options, and I want to make the best of it. Besides, it's a chance to finally get my life together and start my own family."

As she talked more, I realized the full weight of societal expectations, internal beliefs, and the limited choices women had in this country. It was either do or die. Leap in faith or succumb to your fate.

The topic shifted, and she asked me innocently, "What do you want to do?" Her question lingered in the air for a bit, prompting me to reflect on my aspirations.

"Well, I don't want to get married, and you know what? I don't want to be a teacher either. You are probably the first person I am telling this, but I am thinking about leaving this country, actually," I told her in the heat of the moment, but even I could not believe that I said this. Her reaction was swift. She shot me the most twisted look, glaring daggers my way as if I had just uttered something so out of place.

She inched closer, crossed her legs, and after a few minutes, she first said, "Are you crazy? You can't just leave your own country."

Even though I had never felt more determined, something still held me back in that moment from openly announcing my desires. I knew deep down that the path I envisioned for myself was full of challenges, but her strong reaction caught me off guard—yet it wasn't a total surprise. I grappled with her disbelief, trying to find the words to explain my desire for something different beyond the confines of tradition and the regressive rules of this nation. Deep down, even I found it hard to believe that I could take such a significant step.

"I just feel like there's more out there for me," I finally responded, hoping she would understand my inner restlessness and turmoil that yearned for new horizons. I wanted to tell her how much I wanted to fly, taste freedom, and have the chance to embark on new journeys.

She went silent for a while. "You are just dreaming," she said.

"Look, it sounds impossible, and I might not know how, but I'll make it happen, and somehow, I will find a way," I told her. Now that I spelled out to someone that this was what I dreamed of, a newfound courage enveloped me, strengthening my decision. I was still too trusting, but I wanted to leave this country more than anything. After a while, Arie got married, which was an arranged marriage, of course.

The idea of leaving Iran occupied my mind every single day after that. Each morning, I would wake up with thoughts swirling about ways to go, fueled not only by my aspirations but mainly by the formidable situation in the country. However, my reality was difficult because I belonged to a middle-class family; I had no extra money to afford the expensive endeavor of leaving Iran. My desire clashed with the practical constraints of my financial situation. It was a struggle. There were times when I felt I was going nowhere because I was worried about my future so much.

All I knew was that living in a foreign country and dealing with the expenses of travel and everything would require me to put in the effort, so I made the decision to work. I kept this from my mom, not because she would create havoc or she would want to control me, but because independence was unfamiliar territory to her; she was conditioned to be a housewife only, set in her ways, and wanted me to live a safe life she set out for me. I was uncertain how she would take this. I was scared of her abrupt reaction, because she was prone to react a certain way when faced with scenarios related to my desire for independence and freedom.

For that reason, I secretly started job hunting, stumbling upon banks or offices. A few days later, I was finally introduced to an insurance company. I was thrilled when I approached the owner of the insurance company, and he gave the green light for me to start working. The job involved going door-to-door selling insurance. It proved to be one of the most challenging and tiresome tasks for someone as introverted and reserved as I was.

Nevertheless, I persevered and pushed myself above and beyond since, if I wanted my dream to come true, the first step was to acquire money, and I was aware of how limited my employment options were.

On my first day, I was a big ball of nervousness, and anticipation buzzed through my whole body. I entered a car repair shop; the stifling heat made my manteau and scarf unbearable. As beads of sweat dripped down my face, I attempted to explain the benefits of liability insurance.

"Hello, sir. I am here to tell you about liability insurance. With fifty Toman, you can have insurance for a year," I stammered, pulling out paperwork from my bag with a shaky hand.

"What? I can't hear you," the shopkeeper grumbled. He looked grumpy.

I repeated the opening lines that I had rehearsed beforehand, struggling to project my voice. The man instantly looked irritated and fed up with my presence.

"You are too quiet. I can't hear a word you are saying. Show me your papers," he demanded, adjusting his reading glasses on his nose and scrutinizing the documents carefully.

"Ah, you are selling insurance. Girl, you are too quiet. You shouldn't be so shy when selling things, especially insurance. Are you sure you're made for this kind of work? Here, take the fifty Toman. Try to find another job since this doesn't suit you too much," he suggested with a mix of pity and advice.

I felt humiliated and flushed with embarrassment. I mumbled, "Thanks," and left, in a mix of happiness for being able to make my first sale and lingering self-doubt from the shopkeeper's pity.

What if he was right? What if I was not cut for this job? I started wondering. I shook my head, and despite my reservations, decided to give it another shot. I entered the next store with determination. This time, I attempted to raise my voice, hoping the shopkeeper would hear me. I enunciated all my words in a calm manner. My second customer was a short, bald, skinny storekeeper who eyed me skeptically.

"*Khanom* [Madam], you should be ashamed of yourself. Selling is not something a good girl like you should be doing in the first place. Go home. Don't come back. It's a shame for your family." He shut his door in my face.

I walked away, feeling the weight of judgment, stumbled on a step, and fell down on the road. Dusting myself off, I got back up and continued home.

"Where have you been?" my mom questioned when I returned.

"I went to see my friend, Sara," I fibbed, knowing she wouldn't approve of my door-to-door sales efforts.

Despite the fact I was going against the rules of the new government, I was motivated by a bigger dream. The aim was to save money for my goal, but I was disheartened when I faced another day of rejection, with some business owners belittling me and others feeling sorry for me. Negative

45

comments no longer stung as much; my voice grew stronger, and confidence seeped into my pitch.

Time passed, and I became accustomed to people's reactions. My singular focus was on saving money for my dream. As I approached business owners, I gained resilience, selling hundreds of fifty-Toman insurance packages. However, frustration set in when I confronted Mr. Najafi about my unpaid salary.

"It's been a couple of months, Mr. Najafi, and I still haven't received my salary. When will you pay me?" I asked, practically demanding like an employee would, desperation creeping into my voice.

"Oh, Parvin *Khanom*, we don't have enough cash flow to pay you just yet, but if you work harder, we might have enough money in the future," he replied dismissively, ignoring my plea entirely.

"But I need the money now, sir. I can't wait for the future." My voice trembled as I spoke.

"Sorry, girl. You just have to wait," he said coldly.

My teeth clenched as my face heated with anger; I was furious. I realized there was nothing I could do. Disappointed, I quit my job and walked home, uncertain about the next steps.

The setback was disheartening, but my first experience became a steppingstone to explore other avenues and continue pursuing my dreams. So, I applied for other jobs.

Anxiously, I stared at the board covered in job postings. Sheets of paper were pinned to the large panel in the employment office, displaying a myriad of opportunities. My eyes scanned through them, moving from right to left, left to right, up and down. Yet, nothing seemed to align with my qualifications, which were limited to but a high school diploma.

As I sifted through the options, I couldn't help but notice that the majority, if not all, were geared toward men. It was a daunting realization, and the search for a fitting opportunity seemed even more challenging, given the limited options for someone with my qualifications.

"Ah, not even one job posting for me. How am I going to make money?" I was frustrated at that point in my life. Frustrated at the sheer discrimination and hypocrisy that bound women who wanted to work.

"If I stay here longer, grass will grow under my feet, and nothing will happen," I whispered in the employment office.

The lanky, pale-looking guy behind the desk to my left noticed my frustration and signaled me to come closer with a nod and a beckoning finger.

"Take a seat," he said, and I settled into the metal folding chair before him.

He rested his elbow on the desk, his chin on his fist, and idly flipped his shiny, golden pen up and down with his left fingers.

"I've noticed you've been coming here every day for the past couple of weeks. What kind of job are you looking for?" he inquired, eyeing me up and down.

I tried to respond efficiently, but my bone-dry mouth made it difficult for words to escape. Concerned about whether he held any authority or if I had done something wrong gripped me.

Is he a government official? I'm all covered from head to toe. Why did he pick me? I asked myself.

Gathering my remaining courage, I began to speak, "Is there something wrong, sir?"

"Oh, no, madam," he reassured. "I just want to help you. What kind of job are you looking for?" he said with a calm smile.

I hesitated before responding, "Anything would do, as long as it's not a door-to-door sales job."

He leaned in and checked my resume, "With your high school diploma, there's a dentist looking for an assistant. The job just came up, and I haven't been able to post it on the board yet. Would you be interested?"

"Yes, of course," I replied eagerly, grateful for the unexpected turn of events. I couldn't believe this. Finally, things were aligning with my dreams. I hoped for the best and took the job.

On my first day, as I walked into the dentist's office, excitement and nervousness bubbled inside me. I was new and didn't want to leave room for disappointment, so I came early and settled on the gray, metal chair in the waiting room. The scent of medication and alcohol permeating the air filled me with a mixture of eagerness and unease. After about an hour of waiting, a bald man in his late thirties or early forties emerged from one of the doors leading into the waiting area.

"*Salam*, you must be the new assistant," he greeted, extending his hand for a shake.

I hesitated for a moment and then cautiously shook his hand. "You can start tomorrow morning. There is another girl who works here, but she is quitting soon. That's why I need you." He let out a loud laugh.

His laughter echoed, sounding more like a horse's neigh. It was unsettling.

I nodded in response, showcasing my gratitude with my smile. "Yes, of course. Thank you." I was thrilled that this unexpected opportunity had arrived at my gates.

I raced home, bubbling with excitement, eager to share the news about this new job as a dental assistant with my mother. She was already not elated that I was on a job hunt, but I still wanted to share my excitement and achievement.

"*Māmān*, I got a job at a dental office," I squealed with passion, a toothy grin evident on my face.

"The things you do, girl. Your sisters were never into these things. What will people say? They can't afford a living, so their daughter has to work? That is embarrassing. Think about our family's *aaberoo* [saving face]. *Azizam* [dear], are you sure this is the right thing to do?"

It took lots of convincing to get my mother to calm down. I knew she would get aggravated, but I still took time to explain everything. After a month, I proudly waved my first paycheck in her face. Her happiness for me truly blossomed; I could see how proud she was. She even gave me a little peck on my cheek as a reward.

Every day, I would set my alarm for 6:00 a.m. My mom was thrilled to see me waking up so early.

"Good, I don't have to wake you up for your morning prayers. Make sure you do your prayers."

It was the enthusiasm to start the workday that gave me a sense of purpose and a reason to wake up early. It was a sign that if I could do this, I could achieve my dreams too.

My coworkers, Tara and Leena, made the dental office lively. We often found ourselves giggling and laughing for no reason at all. It had been months since I started working there, and on this particular day, as usual, the lab was bustling with equipment to be sterilized and dental models to be poured and sent to the big lab for making dentures and crowns.

I was immersed in my job, focusing on the tasks at hand like usual, when out of nowhere, I felt a hand on my lower back, gently stroking it out of nowhere. I was startled and jumped away from the unfamiliar touch. I turned around to find the dentist standing behind me. I had felt as if I was electrocuted.

"Sorry, I didn't mean to scare you."

I did not dwell on it further and returned my attention to my work.

The dentist, from then onward, would find excuses to touch me. It was all so unexpected and caused an unnerving feeling within; my heart would start racing when he would enter the room. His uncouth behavior disrupted my day-to-day routine. This was the first time as a young woman, any man touched me with an ill intention—other than what usually is just a respectful pat on the back, a father's hug, or an uncle's loving embrace.

It began with random, seemingly casual touches, but then it escalated. The dentist was crossing boundaries. He tried to push past what was acceptable in the office, like caressing my legs. His behavior made me uncomfortable—a shiver would go down my spine each time his clammy hands would touch me. It was such an unpleasant situation to be in. Every time he was near, my entire body would freeze up. I felt highly vulnerable.

Feeling uneasy, I confided in the other girls working in the office. As I shared my experience, they revealed that he had been doing the same to them.

"Yes, he does that to me when he finds me alone. You know he is married and just had a baby," Tara told me.

"Oh, wow, I didn't know he had a kid," I replied, even though I knew a married man displaying this kind of behavior was not surprising at all. I still didn't want to believe it was the reality for certain people. Some men in power hire only female assistants so they can behave in this manner. I started to believe that the assistant before me must have left because of this unruly behavior.

Knowing that the other girls were also enduring similar experiences was a disturbing revelation that confirmed that it wasn't just a one-time incident. I was not aware that I was experiencing workplace harassment, but somehow, talking to them gave me the courage to stand up for myself. One day, I finally gave up and decided not to tolerate his advances anymore.

"No, Doctor, don't touch me; you cannot touch me like that," I protested the next time he tried touching me. My eyes displayed all kinds of anger. I was vexed.

"Why are you upset? This is normal. I am just appreciating your beauty," he said in the most aggravating voice. When I heard him justify his behavior, I wanted to do something profound that could damage his reputation forever.

Still, I was also aware of where I was standing, and living in this country after the revolution had taught me one thing: this could quickly put me in danger.

Later, I talked to Tara about it.

"Tara, I talked to the dentist. I don't know how to stop him," I explained to my friend, frustrated that I couldn't do something about this.

"Yeah, I know. I have tried too. There is nothing we can do to stop him. Who is going to believe us? With this new government, men have all the rights," she said, and I could see how defeated she looked when she talked about it.

"I know, and it is getting worse. Did you hear a woman got stoned just because she claimed she was raped?" Leena added, and that was enough for me to realize and accept the reality we were living in.

I had enough courage to file a complaint against him, but this could easily backfire, and I would be prosecuted for his crimes. That is how the Islamic Republic government worked—one of the hundred reasons I sought a way out.

One day, after working for less than a year as a dental assistant, I couldn't endure it any longer. I stood up and firmly said, pointing a finger at his grim-looking face, "No, you're not allowed to touch me or anyone here."

I slammed the door in his face and left.

I knew then that the dental office was no longer a place for me to work. It was time for me to move on. I was grateful that I had accumulated and set aside sufficient funds for my journey, which I envisioned as my means of reaching my dream.

Where Freedom Lies

Light will someday split you open
even if your life is now a cage.
—HAFIZ

The journey to attain a passport was agonizing. I still remember how the air hung heavy around me, suffocating my conscience. The decision to get a passport was a pivotal step toward my freedom. I stood by the passport office nestled in the affluent region of Shiraz, which was approximately a one-hour bus ride from home.

Upon arrival, the grandeur of the building was overshadowed by the presence of two disgruntled-looking revolutionary guards standing by. They both looked as if they had never experienced even a tiny sprinkle of joy in their lives. It's like happiness saw them from a distance and decided to take a detour. Their threatening machine guns were a stark contrast to my mundane task at hand. Puzzled, I couldn't help but wonder about the need for such a military firearm at a passport office. It made no sense to me.

As I walked closer, my mind raced with queries. I was reluctant to cause any trouble.

Why guns? What are they defending? Who would target a passport office? The unsettling sight lingered as these questions nipped at the back of my mind, demanding answers that remained elusive. As I approached the office, one of the guards stopped me.

"What do you want?" he asked in a rough, raspy voice.

Hesitantly, I replied, "I want to apply for a passport."

I loathed the way his eyes raked all over my body, scrutinizing each and every inch of me before he gestured, "Oh, you can't go inside."

He snapped dismissively and gestured at me to go away because there was a line-up. I looked up at him in surprise, not sure why he had asked me to leave. I couldn't help but wonder if I had done something wrong. Was this another one of their new rules, something that I was unaware of?

With all these new policies emerging out of the blue every few days, it was hard to keep up with all the changes. I decided to muster courage and ask the man why I was denied entry. This would help clear my confusion and let me figure out what was wrong so I would know what to avoid and fix.

"What do you mean I can't go inside?" Frustration welled within me as I asked him. He pointed out, his finger going up and down in the air, gesturing toward my clothing. Eyes scanned me disapprovingly.

"Your attire doesn't meet the standards," he snapped back at me, disapproving of my tone.

"But I'm covered from head to toe," I replied, puzzled.

"Yes, you are covered head to toe, but that's not enough, and you know it. I can see that you are wearing pants, and you know that your manteau should be covering your pants down to your ankle!" he snapped back at me, rejecting my attire and tone.

The guard's response reflected the increasing restrictions on women.

"There isn't a day I'm not stopped for something like a piece of hair showing. Ridiculous," I muttered in defeat, almost to myself.

His furious gaze bore into my skull, and it was warning enough for me to keep my mouth shut. He glared daggers my way. "What did you just say?"

"Nothing, sir." I retreated down the steps and into the corridor, the weight of his intimidating eyes urging me to escape his scrutiny.

At that moment, I realized what kind of dystopian reality I was experiencing. It felt like an endless struggle, where no covering or hiding was sufficient. The nature of this country was regressing to the point that it demanded conformity, an extreme form of compliance only from women, urging us to shield ourselves and cover ourselves in a plethora of clothing. Any hint of skin became a tool for objectification. It wasn't just about a standard; it was about the oppressive state perpetuating the cycle of objectification of women at such a young age.

Walking away briskly, I couldn't shake the realization that mere months under the new government had already ushered in profound limitations for women. The quest for a passport had become more than an excruciating process—it revealed a tightening grip on women's freedom.

With a sad heart, I dragged myself home. I borrowed my mom's longer clothing and oversized scarf and draped myself till I felt like a walking tent, and none of my body was visible. After changing my attire to "suitable requirement," my mom's manteau trailing on the ground, I returned to the passport office and stood in line like a puppet following the script written by societal expectations. The guards, the puppeteers, scanned for any deviation from the imposed standards, any reason to halt my progress.

I moved through the passport office like a marionette in a performance scripted by others, strings tugging me in various directions. The earlier encounter with the guards had left me acutely aware of the consequences women faced for even the slightest transgressions.

I stood in line and waited for my turn. A couple behind me were engaged in a delightful conversation. Then suddenly, the woman made the most terrible mistake known to mankind.

She laughed!

Her laughter echoed through the air, cracking the dead silence. The guard's stern expression portrayed his displeasure and disapproval etched across his face as he attempted to stifle the laughter. The atmosphere tensed as the guard, fueled by misplaced authority, targeted the woman, admonishing her for a crime as trivial as expressing happiness in public.

"You are a woman; women are not supposed to laugh in public," the guard stated boldly, pointing a finger at her.

The husband bravely stepped forward, defending his wife against the unjust accusation, and spoke. "No, it's not her fault. I made her laugh," he asserted, challenging the absurdity of the guard's restrictions.

"Men like you who allow their women to behave this way in public are a disgrace to this country. You will also go to hell along with the woman. *La elaha elallah!*" The guard said, venom dripping from his tongue.

The guard then spat on the side of the stairs and continued, "This kind of behavior turns men on and makes them behave inappropriately. Control your wife, and if you can't, keep her in the house where she belongs."

The couple's faces dropped. I glanced at them, noticing they were as white as ghosts. The wife held her head down and stared at the ground beneath her.

"Yes, sir. I will control her. Please let us go in."

The guard persisted in shaming the husband for letting his wife laugh so brazenly and unabashedly, reinforcing misogyny that sought to suppress the simple act of laughter.

The scene unfolded right in front of me. It made me realize how society suddenly shifted from where freedom reigned and individuals reveled in self-expression and the liberty of doing what they pleased to where even mere laughter was deemed inappropriate for women; women's voices were not allowed to go over a certain decibel. It was just a cruel reminder that marked the stark aftermath of a revolution.

The woman, now cowed and ashamed, lowered her head, embodying the fear instilled by the guard's brutal eyes. Apologies were muttered, not out of genuine remorse, but as a survival instinct in the face of unwarranted authority. Even the men in line were compelled into silence, a silent protest of the unjust curtailment of basic human expressions.

I couldn't stop thinking about our lives before the revolution. The sudden change in beliefs, atmosphere, and traditions was too much to take. I couldn't help but think about when women used to walk on the road freely without a male figure; they used to dance, sing, and have fun, even wear bikinis on the beach. They lived a whole life. It was such a shame that oppression brought about bitter winds of change, and now a woman couldn't even laugh in public.

I recalled one of my friend's friends who had laughed in public; she was taken to jail, where she was brutally mistreated, sexually abused, and raped. Her tragedy and anguish were so intense that she committed suicide after she was released. This story still sends a shiver down my spine. Such gruesome treatment, and for what?

Just laughter?

Outside, through the window, I noticed a pigeon fly, which served as a fleeting reminder of what seemed like an unattainable liberty. Its wings sliced through the air, and for a moment, I yearned to share the same boundless sky, escaping the puppetry imposed by oppressive authorities pulling at my strings.

A pair of wings—that is what I need to fly over and above all this, I thought.

As the couple retreated, their silenced voices echoed the injustice that had crept into a once-liberal society. It was in this brutal silence that I, too, approached the gate, a stark reminder of the cost of defiance and the necessity to conform to this reality. My stoic demeanor concealed the rebellion that simmered within, a subtle act of resistance against the encroaching darkness of injustice.

The mental image of the black and white TV, a relic from when *Little House on the Prairie* painted dreams of unbridled freedom. It was one of my favorite shows. The spirited character of Laura Ingalls had become my refuge. Often, I would feel like mimicking the way she navigated through life. I imagined myself running through fields like that, the wind in my hair, embracing my life with open arms, living freely. She would be a TV character to the rest of the world, but I dreamed of leading a life like hers, and for that to happen, I needed to escape this oppressive regime. As I stood in line for my passport, I thought about her and that one day.

"One day, I will live free. I will feel the freedom Laura felt." I whispered to myself.

Soon, I heard a voice yell. "Next!" an official called, breaking the silence.

I stepped in, my oversized black scarf pulled up to cover my shoulders and all my hair; the only part visible was my face. The bottom of my borrowed black manteau was now dusty gray, dragging on the ground.

There wasn't a trace of a smile on my face—I wiped it away. I could feel the guards looking at me up and down in scrutiny, seeking to find something worth stopping me from going inside, and I wasn't going to give them any reason. So, I followed their instructions.

"You, young girl. Come over here," the guard called.

Hesitantly, I entered the passport office, the room—a solemn space with desks occupied by men, each a gatekeeper to a future beyond my current constraints. Finally, inside, I stood frozen, awaiting instruction like a statue in the center of the room.

Approaching the designated desk, I sat cautiously, pushing forward the forms and photographs. The official peered at me with penetrating eyes, questioning my motives. The room reeked of authority, the weight of judgment heavy in the air. With a shy but determined voice I presented my passport and papers, concealing the trembling within. They questioned my lone travels, a privilege stripped away, as I hastily denied it, fearing the consequences.

"Are you thinking of traveling alone?" he inquired.

"No, sir. I want to have a passport for the future. In case my family wants to travel," I responded, my words measured and careful.

As the barrage of questions and answers proceeded, they demanded a male figure should accompany me. I explained my father's passing, only to face subsequent demands for a brother or uncle. My father's mention cut deep, a painful reminder of a loss that had left an incredible void. I gave them further information about my family. I only had sisters; they demanded my uncle next, and I had to inform them that all my uncles lived in other cities. Silence followed, and after a sigh, I told them about my brothers-in-law. I named one, and he was summoned.

The absence of a mother's consent felt like a strange and bitter reminder of how little a woman's say mattered in legal proceedings.

Thankfully, my brother-in-law was more open-minded. He was like a friend to me, so he understood. He signed the papers, granting reluctant approval to a journey that challenged the oppressive system.

The official examined the forms, his gaze penetrating through full eyebrows, his mouth contorting like a horse's. "All right, leave these forms here and return in a month to see if your passport is ready."

"Really?" I asked giddily, constraining my happiness. The impulse to smile widely bubbled up, but I stifled it. The fluttering wings of the pigeon mirrored my anticipation within.

Not now, I told myself. *Wait.*

"Thank you, sir," I uttered with relief; my beating heart served as my compass. The passport, a symbol of freedom, lay in the hands of distant officials, and my journey toward a future unknown had only just begun.

A month later, when I returned to the passport office and received my passport, I knew that my documents were reluctantly accepted, and a surge of joy threatened to break free, only to be stifled by the persistent fear of repercussions.

As I exited the passport office, a conflicted dance of emotions played within me. I was almost smiling, almost laughing, but also, the specter of oppression hung heavy on my shoulders. The injustice of a system that sought to clip the wings of autonomy and self-expression was palpable.

Each step forward felt like I was walking on a tightrope. I just needed to tread my way carefully to the end, where my freedom lay.

Faith

Faith is an oasis in the heart which will never
be reached by the caravan of thinking.
—KHALIL GIBRAN

I sat on the edge of my bed in the privacy of my room and gently cradled my brand-new passport. My fingers held the weight of the document as I ran my hand over the engraved seal, feeling the rigid texture of the passport cover.

My eyes started to well up.

I felt elated, yet disbelief had a tight grip on me. My fingers gently brushed against the adhesive label on the front, noticing the label had covered the original passport cover that had Pahlavi's Lion, Sword, and Sun emblem. A little hint of resentment found its way into my heart.

It was hard to believe that all my dreams were about to come true—the dreams I worked so hard for, the dreams I couldn't fulfill in this country, the dreams revolution had tried to suffocate. I felt like an eagle about to spread her wings and take off. My heart felt like it was exploding with joy.

I have never felt so alive as I did in that moment.

With every stroke of my fingertips against the stamp, I felt myself getting one step closer to my destiny. I savored the moment. Terrified at the prospect of living alone in a strange land all by myself, I was apprehensive but determined. Bombarded by emotions, the one that resurfaced the most was pure bliss, which enabled me to embark on this journey.

My passport was the ticket to the land of freedom. I was finally going to be free.

Now, the only thing that nipped at the back of my brain was how I would break this news to my precious mother. Having known her since the beginning of my time, one thing was sure—she would not take it well, but I had to break it to her someday and somehow. She has to know about my future plans, although I already had an excuse ready. I was going to use my further education as my primary reason for leaving. I knew she would find attending the university to be somewhat logical.

She really doesn't have to know the details of why I desperately want to leave, I thought.

When I thought of America, I could see myself building a life of my own, finding myself, catering to my needs. America would only provide me with some of what I needed; I knew I would face obstacles when I landed there, but at least I'd have freedom of choice.

I just had to figure out how to break the news to my mom. One fine morning, with butterflies in my stomach, I built up the courage for the deed. It was a warm spring day, a sunny warmth cut through by a chilly breeze. Mom had spread the rug over the wooden cot out in the yard. There she was, sitting on the rug, cleaning out the herbs for dinner. I breathed out in profound distress.

I walked into the yard and stood in front of her.

"Move, girl. You are blocking the sun," she grumbled, immersed in the herbs; she didn't even look up. A brisk wind brushed against me, cooling down my nervous, sweaty body as I stood persistently.

"*Māmān*, I wanted to talk to you about something," I said hesitantly, fidgeting my fingers, hoping by ignoring what she asked me to do, she would leave what she was tending to and pay attention to me. She placed the tray full of herbs down and looked at me.

"What is it? What do you want to say?"

I took a deep breath and blurted, "Well, *Māmān*, I want to move to America."

Her eyes locked onto mine. I held my breath as she stared at me for quite some time. I could see disbelief in her eyes, confusion etched upon her face.

She huffed. "Is this a joke? Go clean the dishes. I will have to make dinner soon." She dismissed me and returned to catering to the herbs.

My words came out shaky. "No, *Māmān*, I am dead serious. I want to go to university and continue my education abroad," I insisted.

She scooted over so I could sit beside her and have a proper conversation. She turned her head toward me and stared at me in a way I had never seen. Unsure of her unfamiliar gesture, I sat frozen beside her.

She shook her head. Her sharp gaze pierced straight through the core of my determination.

"Don't worry about the university, Parvin *Jaan*. Soon, you will have a good proposal, like your sisters, and he will be a good man for you to marry." Her nonchalant tone to my revelation was agonizing.

Before I approached her, I had the whole conversation planned in my mind. I knew what she might say. Even though I have repeatedly made it clear how I felt about marriage every time she brought up the prospect of marriage, I couldn't stop my anger.

"*Na, na*. I don't want to get married. I want to go to America to do my higher studies."

I stood my ground this time. I noticed a shift in my mother's eyes. Her demeanor changed entirely, like a thunderstorm was about to strike.

Parvin, be prepared, I told myself.

She sighed and sat upright. She hugged her knees to her chest. Her lips were pursed with frustration. I feared what she was going to say next.

Suddenly, she hit the back of one hand with her other hand hard enough to make her skin turn red.

"You are dreaming, my dear. A young, Muslim girl leaving the country alone …? How can you even think that? You must be out of your mind! You have no money or man to protect you. Who would pay for your living expenses there, huh? Answer me?" she scrunched up her nose, which used to make me laugh but didn't seem funny anymore.

Arms crossed and annoyed, I replied. "I can do it on my own, *Māmān*. Cousin Moe did it a couple of years ago. Why can't I do it?"

"But Moe is a man, and you are a girl. There's a big difference. Can't you see that? Plus, where will you get money from? *La elaha elallah*. You will have us bankrupt and lose face in front of people," she warned me with frustration.

The idea of a man traveling alone and exploring his individuality was worth appreciating, but when the same thing applies to a girl, all hell breaks loose. This disparity was one of the many reasons I wanted to escape.

I was glad that I saved a lot from the jobs I did. I had enough money saved up that would help me cover my expenses abroad. I enlightened my mother about the money situation and tried to assure her about how I'd be able to manage.

My reasoning couldn't convince her. I could feel her concern after our talk. Her state of distress made me feel selfish, yet I wanted my freedom. I was desperate for it but also wanted my mother's approval. I wanted her to send me off with a big smile and contented heart—but that seemed merely impossible.

My mother, throughout the day, looked like a big ball of anxiety. I knew her and how angsty she could get. She was worried to the point that she decided to call my sisters and their families over on the weekend to have a little discussion. She paced around and took longer breaths. That was a clear sign that she was afraid. Her gaze remained watery throughout the day. She kept busy preparing dinner and often talking under her breath with a big sigh or a huff. I knew the news would affect her, but I didn't realize it would be to this degree. My mother was a perfectionist, but I saw her get this fidgety, as if she was having a hard time staying still.

When my sisters and their families were huddled around, she broached the subject again. My sisters looked at me, dumbfounded at the new piece of information.

"Where do you even want to go?" My mom asked again. Agitation dripped from her body language. I understood the root of her reaction; she was a profoundly concerned mother. After my departure, she'd be alone; maybe that prospect also scared her.

My sister Arie saw the banter between *Māmān* and me and decided to chime in.

"Girls shouldn't entertain such thoughts. Who knows what could happen to you out there? God forbid anything terrible." Displeasure was evident from her tone as she eyed me with complete skepticism.

"You'll regret it forever," Azita, another one of my sisters, objected.

I gazed up at my mother. She seemed satisfied with my sisters' disapproving stance, as if that's the reason she held this sudden meeting to make me question my choices.

"*Azizam*, can you really leave *Māmān* and go away?" Zoe, my other sister, said, trying to emotionally blackmail me into compliance. I felt like the spotlight was on me as I was interrogated about my future livelihood in America. I didn't want to go into detail about why I wanted to leave, because once I started with the extensive list of reasons behind this decision, I wouldn't be able to stop myself.

"I disagree with you leaving the country. Just forget about it," one sister's husband interfered. They seemed bewildered by my decision, just like the rest.

Bombarded with impromptu advice and admonishments, I felt terribly misunderstood among my own people. The best I could do was leave them be and continue my journey.

"Everything you need is here at home," my sister said. I rolled my eyes, feeling defeated. There was no way I could reason with their blinkered remarks.

"You have a roof over your head and warm food in your belly. What more could you possibly want?"

The more they pushed, the more determined I became, insisting on my decision.

After a while, their voices became just a background noise echoing through the house. All I was thinking about was my passport tucked under my clothes in my cupboard, which sustained me with deep joy. I had an epiphany then and there about how much unwavering trust I needed in myself because no one in this room would offer any. I was the one who was going to embark on this new chapter of my life, and it was only possible due to my own strength and determination. A long road to self-discovery and actualization lay ahead of me.

I was terrified but determined.

A few days after that conversation, I took a stroll to one of my favorite bazaars: Vakil, an ancient bazaar built around the period of the Zand dynasty. In the bazaar, side-by-side adjacent shops showcase Persian rugs adorned with exquisite and elaborate traditional designs. Only a few stores had merchandise other than Persian rugs. As I passed the *Chahar-soo* intersection of Bazaar, I couldn't help but look for my dad's old store, now owned by a stranger. A wave of sadness sat in my heart.

"I miss *Bābā*," I whispered to myself. Standing in the corner of the intersection, I find myself captivated by his shop as memories from the past unfold in my mind like movie scenes.

The middle school made me feel like a grownup. It had just been a few months since I started grade seven. Learning to navigate my way to and from school was a challenge in the beginning, but I soon felt comfortable and confident enough to daydream during my forty-five-minute walk home after school.

It was a cold, winter afternoon, and my walk on a day like that felt much longer than it really was. The streets along my path were very quiet.

A stream of muddy water from the rainfall the night before was running through the *gully* (lane) parallel to the sidewalks, carrying dry leaves along. The dark clouds in the sky indicated it was about to rain.

I hate this type of weather. It makes me sad, I thought.

The wind was blowing my gray uniform and lifting it away, uncovering my bare knees above my navy, knee-high socks, making my legs cold and shaky.

I lifted my hands to warm up my face and nose, but it just made my bare fingers freeze to numbness. The air in front of my face turned to steam as I tried to warm up my hands with the warm air from my lungs.

Delicious, almost palpable thoughts of sitting on the living room floor covered with patterned Persian rugs, making a nest with my mom's checkered, wool blanket, and sticking my frozen face and toes in front of the pale-green kerosene heater in the middle of the room, kept me walking faster toward home.

Mom always had a steeped Darjeeling tea mixed with sour orange blossoms picked from the tree in our yard, ready to warm me up from the inside on cold days. The room would fill with the aroma of tea. I imagined a cup of her tea melting the icicles inside my tummy and warming me all the way through. With these soothing thoughts in my head, I walked home faster and faster.

Closer to home, the narrower alleys created by tall walls surrounding the houses protected me more from the harsh, cold breezes. Occasionally, a bicycle or a person passed by. The old sycamore tree in the middle of the bazaar always mesmerized me. Its trunk was wide enough for four men to stretch their arms around and still not be able to reach each other's hands. I took a deep breath as I walked through the bazaar, inhaling the aroma of the herbs sold by the shopkeepers. The smell of kebab from the kebab house made me hungry.

I hope Māmān *made kebab for dinner,* I thought.

The roads were winding and narrow like snakes. I liked the new house in our neighborhood with its white walls, a blue metal door, and windows on the right. The sound of music coming through their open windows each time I passed by made me happy, and I wished we had that in our home.

It had been a long time since I had heard any music played on the radio at home. With Dad's illness, he had no patience to hear music. One more turn to the right, and there I was, in my home alley. As I drew closer to home, I noticed a coffin on the side of the road beside the door to our home. My heart skipped a beat.

What is going on? I thought.

I knew it meant someone had died. *Maybe the coffin belongs to one of the neighbors,* I hoped. I shivered at the thought of a dead body in the box. Horrified by the thought that one of our neighbors might be lying dead in the box, I pulled myself as far away from it as I could.

The entrance door to the long hallway leading to our courtyard was surprisingly wide open. It was unusual for our family to leave the door in the tall, protective wall surrounding the house open.

"Close the door. We don't want strangers to walk into the yard without notice. Make sure the door closes tight," my mom would say.

Pulling away from the coffin by the door, watching in case a dead body jumped out at me, I cautiously tiptoed inside the long and dark hallway leading to our courtyard. I could hear people talking and women crying. I peeked into the yard. Astonishingly, lots of people clothed in black were gathered in separate groups. Some were crying. Some were talking quietly.

I took one step and the next step down into the courtyard. I looked around to find my mother. There were some familiar faces in the crowd whom I hadn't seen for a long time, some faces I had never seen.

What are these people doing here? Where is Māmān? I thought.

I pushed through the crowd to find her. Instead, I found all three of my sisters, all in black, sitting on the wooden cot in the courtyard, crying. Zoe, my sister, had passed out. People were gathered around, trying to wake her up.

My heart was fluttering in my chest like the wings of the sparrow I had once held in my hands. Something bad had happened, and I didn't want to know what.

I pulled myself away and watched my sisters cry and wail out loud. The pain deep in their eyes felt like a knife in my chest.

I was invisible. See-through. Not even my sisters could see me. My mother was in the kitchen, dressed in all-black and covered in a black *chador*. I ran to her and hung on tight to her waist. I could feel the beating of my heart against her torso.

"What is happening, *Māmān*? Why are these people in our house? Why is everyone crying?"

Mom didn't answer.

I was relieved because I knew the story wasn't going to be the sweet fairytale I would prefer to hear.

"Follow me," Mom said.

I followed her through the yard. The rooms surrounding the courtyard were filled with people chattering and milling about.

She turned around and signaled me to go with her up the stairs to one of the rooms and to a walk-in closet. The cozy, dark space in the closet felt safe. Her gaze was on the floor, trying to avoid eye contact. I could see her teary eyes filled with sadness. Her face was pale, the corners of her mouth drooping down.

"What is happening, *Māmān*? Why are all these people in our home? Are you all right?"

She let out a big sigh as if that little closet also allowed her to breathe.

Without answering, she pulled out a folded square of black Georgette fabric from her special leather suitcase and handed it to me.

"Go to the madam tailor's home and ask her to sew a *chador* for your sister Zoe."

"But why?"

"Just go to the tailor's and ask her to sew the *chador* and stay there until it's ready, and then bring it back home. Now run, run, go on."

I dashed through the alleys and passed *Kal-Khalil*'s ice cream shop.

He yelled out loud, "Are you all right?"

I was proud that my mom trusted me to give me such an important task. I shouted back, "Yes, just going to the tailor."

Puzzled by Kal-Khalil's concerns for me, I thought, *Hmm, he never asked me if I was all right before. Why is he asking me today?*

Yet, I didn't pay much attention to that. I had an important mission to accomplish. I continued running.

I ran through the cobblestone alleys, past the old *Baghdadi* mosque where my mom sometimes took me to pray, and passed the old, abandoned *Abdaar Khaaneh* aqueduct.

When I finally arrived at madam tailor's home, she welcomed me with a big hug. *Weird*, I thought; I had never seen her so loving before. Once we settled down in her sewing room, I handed her the fabric and relayed my mother's instructions.

"Come. Come and have some tea and biscuits. You must be hungry. How are things at home?" she asked with a kind smile.

"My house is full of strange people, and I don't know why!" I wailed.

"Your dad is sick; maybe they are visiting your dad."

I shrugged with my shoulders raised to my ears and my lower lip extending out.

"When did you see your dad last? How was he doing?"

"I haven't seen him for a couple of weeks. He is always in his room, but I can hear him moaning from the yard. Mom said I should be quiet and stay away because he is so sick."

"Oh, that's too bad. Your father is a good man. Don't you forget that."

"Yes, madam tailor."

Surprised by all her attention to my dad, I still didn't clue into what she was trying to tell me, or perhaps I just didn't want to know.

Within an hour, my sister's *chador* was sewn.

"Here you go. Take this back to your mom and give her my regards."

I ran back home with the folded *chador* in my hand. By the time I got home, I was out of breath. To my surprise, there were still lots of people in our house. Mom took the new *chador* and gave it to my sister, who had just revived from her fainting spell. Zoe's eyes were puffed up and red.

Sorrow filled up every corner of the house. Even the chickadees in the old, sour-orange tree chirped differently. Sadness was pouring from their delicate, little beaks, warning of the lonely, sad days ahead.

The doors and windows to my father's room were wide open. My view was blocked by women and their tent-like *chadors*. I peeked through and between the crowds, only to see he was missing from his room. His bed was still there in the corner of the room, but he wasn't in it. The blanket on the floor where he used to smoke cigarettes was gone too. The dusty mirror on the shelf reflected the smoke-covered room, but no sign of my father.

I had no tears, but my chest felt devastated by a tornado of emotions. *My dad is no longer here.*

"What is going to happen to him?" I yelled out loud, but my voice felt like it was too far away from the ears of adults around me. I heard no answer.

With her teary eyes, my mom guided me outside the house as we followed the coffin through the alleys.

Carrying your beloved's body in a coffin on men's shoulders and walking to the cemetery was a tradition. The belief was the more people that gather and pray for the deceased, the more his or her sins on this earth would be wiped away, and the deceased would enter heaven.

My gaze was on the wooden box carried in front of us by four men holding it on their shoulders.

What if it is all a mistake, and he is still alive in the wooden box?

"Let my dad out of the box!" I wanted to scream, but my voice was stuck in my throat.

Nourooz, the Persian New Year, was coming soon. It would be the first day of spring, when everyone was all excited and preparing for the new year. People will be dressing up in their brand-new clothes. Children would be excited to receive their monetary gifts from the elders in the family, but this year would be different for our family. *Nourooz without Bābā.* I wondered how empty and bleak it would be.

Each *Nourooz*, I would dress in my brand-new clothes and shoes to go to my dad's room on the morning of the new year. I would be ready early in the morning before everyone else was up.

"Can I go to *Bābā*'s room now, *Māmān*?"

"No, you have to wait. He is still asleep."

Impatiently, I would wait, making sure my new dress didn't get dirty and my new shoes were spotless. Wiping them occasionally with my hands, I'd make sure they were shining.

After my mom would bring back my dad's empty breakfast tray to the kitchen, I knew this was a sign that he was ready for visitors. Dressed up in our brand-new clothes, my sisters and I would follow our mother to his room.

I loved the squeaking sound my shoes made when I walked. That was the sound of brand-new shoes.

Mom would sit in the corner of the room on the carpeted floor and guide us one by one to see him. As the youngest of four daughters, I was the first in line.

I would go forward and kneel on the blanket on the floor where he'd be sitting.

"Happy New Year, *Agha Jaan*." I would say.

"Happy New Year to you, too, little girl." he would respond lovingly.

With a pause and shyness, I'd ask, "Can I have my *eidee* [gift of money], please?"

"Not until you give me a kiss."

I'd kiss him on the cheeks. *Smack*.

"No, this one doesn't count. It didn't have any sound. Here, I'll show you how it is done." Dad would lean in and kiss my cheek with a dramatic sound. "Muah."

His spiky, short, gray beard used to prick the skin on my cheeks. The warmth of his skin and the intensity of the smell of cigarettes on his breath made me feel loved.

"Now, you try."

This would go on until he finally agreed I got it right. Then he'd pull out crisp, unfolded paper money and hand it to me.

"Here you go. Don't buy junk food with it. Get some ice cream. You can share it with me, too, if you want. Hahaha!"

I would grab the money with sparkling eyes and dash out of his room, giddy with happiness.

The heavy sound of the funeral prayer snapped me back into the present moment. Holding my mom's black *chador*, I followed hundreds of people who were following the coffin my father was sleeping in.

Men were chanting,

> *"Allah-o Akbar"*
> *"Laellaha ellallah"*

I had heard this chant before as people carried their beloved's body to the cemetery. It was the song of death and sorrow.

In disbelief, all I could think about was my dad being in a wooden box.

Thoughts of the way he used to pound the iron knocker on our tall, wooden door when he came home from his shop played like a movie in front of my eyes and gave me assurance and safety.

Knock, knock, knock, and then a pause and *knock, knock.*

My frozen hands and toes made it hard to hold on to my mother's *chador*, to feel her protection and catch up with her.

"Fridays are the day dead people are waiting for their families to visit them," she said. *It is creepy*, I thought.

Nowhere in my wildest dreams did I imagine, one day, my father would be waiting for me to visit him in the graveyard on Fridays.

My heart started racing as we approached the cemetery. Everything became more real.

I hadn't seen him in his last days. Now, he was all bundled up in white burial clothing while a couple of guys slowly lowered him into the pre-dug grave. My heart sank. I wanted to reach out and stop them.

No, you can't do that to my bābā! *You can't put my* bābā *in a scary hole in the ground.*

Everyone was chanting and praying.

My mother wiped her tears with the edge of her *chador*. I had seen her tears before, but I had never seen her wailing this way.

I backed up as far as I could, tripping and trampling over the graves. I stood as far away as I could in disbelief. I could not see my father, my rock, now in the ground and disappearing forever.

I wanted everyone to disappear and let go of my father. Instead, I watched men one by one, shovel in hand, throwing earth on him.

The frozen voice in my throat yelled out, "Don't do that; maybe he will wake up!"

Our home wasn't the same ever again. Dad's room lost the smell of cigarettes and his aftershave shortly after he was gone. Mother was always struggling to figure out how to manage her responsibilities. Suddenly, there was a huge void in our lives, which nothing could ever fill back up.

I snapped out of my headspace as the shopkeeper behind me yelled out, *"Khanom chi mikhay bekhari"* (Madam, what do you want to buy)?

"Sorry, sir. Nothing," I replied and walked away.

As I passed the only luggage store in the bazaar, my eyes were magically drawn to this big, ethereal, brown suitcase. My heart leaped toward the bag. That's how beautiful it was. I had money saved to buy some travel goods, and this would be an excellent start. I stood in front of the store with determination. When something appealed to you at that time, you had to point to it from outside. Entering the store without the intention of buying was frowned upon.

"Sir, can you show me that suitcase please?"

The shopkeeper took a careful glance at me and asked my age.

"I'm eighteen, sir, and I'd like to buy the suitcase."

He still looked skeptical, as if I were lying. "Are you sure you are of legal age?" he asked.

"Yes, I am," I answered proudly.

"How would you be able to afford it?" he questioned me.

"I have the money for it, don't worry, so can I please take a closer look at it?" I persisted.

"Tell me you are a hundred percent sure before I bring it down," he asked again. He looked confused. I was frustrated by his mistrust of me.

Even the simple shopkeeper doesn't trust my ability, I thought.

After a barrage of questions and showing him my money, it took me quite some time to convince him that I wanted to buy the suitcase. Finally, with that beautiful bag in hand, I made my first big purchase on my path to freedom. At home and in the privacy of my room, I stroked its surface, and right away, I felt her gentle, soft, feminine energy, and that's where I decided my big, brown suitcase was female. I placed this magnificent bag on my bed and referred to Big Brown as "her" because that felt right.

I grazed my hand on the top and felt a wave of comfort and gratification wash over me, but mostly, I felt powerful.

Big Brown conveyed a sense of accomplishment; she gave me strength, and her presence quickly morphed my anxiety into complacency. Then, gently, I placed her under my bed, where she would be safe.

Soon, my big, brown suitcase became an unwavering form of support that brought tranquility to my life. She restored my faith in my decision and compelled me to take the risk for the sake of my freedom.

After all, if I wouldn't put faith in myself, who else would?

7

Vulnerable

Vulnerability sounds like truth and feels like
courage. Truth and courage aren't always
comfortable, but they're never weakness.
—BRENÉ BROWN

"No girl from our family has ever traveled on her own anywhere, let alone Tehran. Tehran is a dangerous place for a girl. It's so crowded and busy. I can't let you go there," my mother protested when I broke the news about Tehran. I was not at all surprised by my family's outburst. In fact, I was now used to their constant grievances about anything related to me leaving the country.

My sisters were huddled around me, trying hard to interrogate and scare me so I would step back from my decision. I just didn't know why it was so difficult for them to understand that I didn't want a life like theirs. I obviously didn't say this out loud out of courtesy.

"Why are you so hardheaded? Don't you see we want the best for you? We are ensuring nothing bad happens to you!" one of my sisters said.

"I am not happy with you, and you know what this means? It means God is not happy with you, and when God is unhappy with you, you will not go to heaven. Now, go do what you want to do," my mother scoffed as she made a sad face and admonished me. She was trying her best to get me to stay.

I stayed in my place and let my family vent, but inside, I was seething with frustration. It was easier to talk to them once they had cooled off. I love my family with the depth of my heart, but I was determined to follow my dreams. Marriage and that life, with all its restrictions, were not a part of my dream. Everything beyond my freedom seemed like an annoying background noise—nothing but a distraction. I didn't want to hurt my sisters' feelings, but their voices of negativity soared higher within that distraction. It was true. I had never traveled anywhere alone. Only wealthy families and men would dare to dream of living in a foreign country. Naturally, thoughts of what might happen to me while traveling for twelve to fourteen hours were frightening. The voices inside my head kept me up at night. I was only human in the end, and their admonishments were beginning to get to me.

What if my family is right? What if I get lost or kidnapped and raped! I pondered, then shook my head quickly, putting all the terror-filled thoughts aside. I needed to be strong for my own sake, for my dream. If my determination dwindled now, I couldn't chase my goals.

I paid zero attention to my family's deterrent attempts to dull my ambition. I wrote a letter to my cousin Moe, who lived in California, about admissions opening there.

> *Dear Cousin Moe,*
>
> *I hope you are doing fine and having a great time in America. I bet you are enjoying your weekend, too. I wanted to write this letter to make sure about the admissions. Can you please send me an application form so I can apply to join the University of California?*
>
> *I hope to see you soon.*
>
> *Sincerely Parvin.*

I waited for his response patiently. A couple of weeks later, a mailman arrived, and I ran toward the door like a roadrunner. My hands were shaking as I struggled to open the mail. The contents of this letter would decide my future. It would determine if I was destined for the fruit of liberation or if my fate would still be in the hands of *mullahs* ruling in this country.

I was on cloud nine when I opened the envelope. I realized that it was indeed a university application—that much I could tell. The only downside was that it was written entirely in English. Despite my best efforts to comprehend the words and sentences, no matter how hard I tried, I couldn't understand a word.

One of my other cousins had taken extracurricular English classes, so her English was much better than mine. I took the letter to her house in hopes of translation.

"Wow, I thought I could read some English, but I can't understand one line of what the form says," I said in frustration.

"Yeah, the English they teach us in high school here is good for nothing," she replied.

She grabbed the dictionary from her shelf, and we both looked for words we had never heard of—the words that sounded too foreign to us. We struggled, but after three days, we managed to finally decode all the pages with the help of a dictionary.

I filled the form out and sent it back. Now, I had to wait patiently for the university to answer. My days were filled with anxiety, and my nights were sleepless, waiting for an answer; I didn't want to be disappointed. Life was already full of disappointments; I just wanted a mere crumb of happiness and hope.

Finally, after a couple of weeks, the mailman handed me a US-stamped letter with English writing on the back. I grabbed the letter. My heart was beating fast, and it felt like it was going to leap out of my chest, my hands trembling and my palms sweaty, yet I managed to tear open the envelope haphazardly.

It was my university admission. My application was accepted. Tears of happiness streamed down my face as I collapsed to my knees in the courtyard, overwhelmed with pure joy. This was monumental news. I could not believe it. It felt so surreal.

It was finally happening—the new chapter of my life.

I pressed the letter against my chest. "Thank you, thank you, thank you, God." I cried.

I was elated with the new turn of events in my life. After the revolution struck, I felt lost in the thick crowd of radicalism. I felt misplaced; I forgot to laugh, breathe, and cherish, but I also was grateful for becoming empowered enough to make such prodigious life choices that led me to the path of freedom.

I often wonder if I would ever make these bold choices if life were easier on me as a young woman!

I was excited but also frightened at the prospect of traveling alone to Tehran. I had to get my visa from the American embassy located in the heart of Tehran. It was going to be a long journey. I needed to familiarize myself with the whereabouts of Tehran.

There were days when I would recall my family's reprimanding voices. I might have been beyond ecstatic and determined with how my life turned out, but I was also petrified to my very core. I kept pushing those thoughts away at the back of my brain in order to move forward. If I managed to get to this point all on my own, I'd be able to manage it in the future too. There was no point in wondering about "what ifs," I tried to convince myself. So, I concentrated on trusting myself and looking ahead.

The first step was to get a place to stay in Tehran. I suddenly remembered that one of my cousins, Lily, lived in Tehran. Even though I had only met her once or twice in my life in Isfahan, a city where my parents were born and bred, I decided to write her a letter about my plans and see if she'd agree to let me crash at her place for a while.

I began to write her a letter with high hopes.

Dear Lily,

Hello! You might not remember me, but I am your cousin Parvin from Shiraz. We met in Isfahan a couple of times. I do not know if you remember or not. I want to apply for a visa to the United States of America, so I have to travel to Tehran. I would like to know if I can stay with you for a while. Please let me know if it would be appropriate. I'll be waiting for your response.

Sincerely, your cousin, Parvin.

P.S. If yes, also send me your address, please.

A week later, I finally got a response from Lily.

"The door to my house is always open for you," she wrote in her letter.

I was relieved; she was excited to see me again and accepted my request with open arms.

Reality was setting in, and I felt unprepared for this significant leap. Up until now, I had been shielded in the safety of home and my mother's care. I began to plan my journey. I had to be aware of everything if I was going to travel alone. I bought myself a map of Tehran so it would be easier for me to navigate.

"Wow, Tehran is huge." I spread the map onto the floor of my room. I traced my index finger on the lines of the map. My finger followed the pathways, the alleys, and the streets. The intricacy of the map almost made me feel dizzy working my way through it. The city was complex. It was definitely the kind of place a person like me would get lost.

"Aha! There it is—Lily's place." I said, giddy like a child who'd just found Waldo. I kept a red marker on the side and marked Lily's place with X.

Now, it was my turn to find the embassy. A loud, joyful shriek escaped me when my finger landed on the American embassy. I clamped my mouth shut so I didn't upset my mother with my uncontrollable, squeaky voice. I marked the American embassy with a red heart.

Then, I drew a dotted line over the streets of Tehran, taking me from Cousin Lily's place to the American embassy. I sighed in relief when one more conquest was resolved. Now, it was just me and this new journey that stared directly at me.

My eyes darted to Big Brown lying peacefully in the corner. I felt content with her presence. It was remarkable how a lifeless thing could stir up so much emotion in me. She brightened my day; I could feel her encouraging me. I could feel her being proud of me. I could feel her inspire me.

She was my faithful companion from the start.

The next few days went by quickly. Anxious and excited, I woke up on the day of travel. My mom was already up for her morning prayers. Unable to persuade me to change my mind, all she could do was pray for me.

The slight twitch of her eyes, as she prayed for my safety and security, showed how concerned she was. I felt a pang of ache right in my chest when I thought of leaving my mom. I loved her dearly, but sacrifices had to be made.

She glanced at me, eyes narrowed. "Get up and do your prayers. God will protect you when you pray," she instructed, and I obeyed her.

I jumped off the bed, washed up, and prayed; I knew that made her happy. Her enamored eyes clouded my spirit with guilt, yet the sorrow in her eyes reflected the years of pain she'd been through.

In a way, I was doing this for her. I was breaking the generational curse of the women of my family.

It ends here. It ends with *me*.

She thought I wouldn't notice her subtle glances. Her meaningful hand on the top of my head was her way of blessing me. She was worried, but I could also see a gleam of pride in her eyes. No woman in our family could do what I was about to do.

By freeing myself, I was freeing the innocent child in her. The child who had been suffocated when she was merely eight years old. I was doing this for that eight-year-old girl.

After breakfast, we said our goodbyes. I held her in my embrace for longer than I imagined. I headed toward the bus station, holding my big, brown suitcase in one hand. It was a crisp fall morning when I arrived at the bus station way too early, hoping to get a good seat beside a woman.

"Women are harmless. Try to find a seat beside a woman," Mom's advice rang through my mind like a morning bell.

Autumn was here to stay. The sun bathed the world golden as the sky was vast; infinite blue hovered above me. The chilly gust of a breeze felt soothing to my cold nose. My long-sleeved manteau pants and scarf were a careful wall between me and my body, making sure none of my curvature was visible even to the critical eye. My face was the only part of my body that allowed me to be exposed to the natural light. I did not let the weight of my oppression humble me.

I looked at the clouds that appeared as tufty pillows. I breathed in the cool autumn air as it took some pressure off my shoulders, and I trod ahead like a woman on a mission.

After waiting impatiently for a couple of hours, the bus finally pulled in front of me. The driver sitting at the front hollered loudly.

"All passengers to Tehran, you can get on the bus now."

There were a few people huddled around behind me. Everyone rushed and pushed to get on first. By the time I was able to board, the only available seat was at the back of the bus beside a bearded man. At least I was able to find a spacious compartment for Big Brown.

"So much for trying to find a seat beside a woman," I whispered to myself in deprecation.

"Sir, may I sit here?" I asked gently. Making sure I had a neutral and blank expression on my face so he wouldn't misconstrue it.

The bearded man ogled me up and down. He had an uncouth look on his face as though he tasted something bitter. His eyes were full of contempt. He didn't say anything, but his expressions told a different story. I could sense what he wanted to say. Something along the lines of "How dare you travel alone!"

He shifted aside without saying anything. Thankfully.

I placed my belongings under the seat before me, then hesitantly settled into my seat and let out a loud exhale as I sat down.

I peeked over the seat in front to see the passengers before me. The bus was crowded. I noticed how there were only a few women on the bus, and they were all accompanied by a man. Their gaze down, body fully clothed. The usual.

My heart sank a little to see women outnumbered by men in public spaces. Being the only woman traveling alone among the passengers created a dilemma inside me. I started doubting my dreams. Confliction clouded me. I began to panic. My hands trembled. My leg bounced.

"Maybe I shouldn't be here. Maybe it is all a mistake," I muttered to myself, experiencing a sudden realization. "What was I doing here?"

I didn't want to succumb to a panic attack, so I gathered myself and decided to do a little breathing exercise. These were just negative thoughts trying to take over me.

Deep breath, Parvin. Deep breath, I guided myself. *There you go.*

When my breathing was brought back to normal, I took a moment to realize that I made it to a bus all on my own and I was there to collect my visa. A new wave of pride hit me as I looked back at my journey.

Maybe the guy beside me doesn't have any bad intentions. Maybe his face is deformed, and he always looks like this, or maybe he just has that constipated look, I tried to reason with myself.

I swiftly shifted to the far end of my seat, so no part of my body came in contact with his.

As the bus crossed one block, I started daydreaming about my life abroad and how perfect things would be in America. I started fantasizing about what outfits I would wear every day for the university. I wouldn't be liable to wear a *hijab* anymore. I would finally be able to ride a bicycle to university.

Occasionally, the bearded man's snore would interrupt my fairy tale dream.

The little, white house on green land with white picket fences all around it. An extensive swing set and tall, old trees in the distance; coffee shops, libraries, and food trucks were all around.

It was indeed the land of freedom. My sweet dream played in my mind like a movie. This kept me motivated and encouraged me so I wouldn't lose hope like I almost did a few minutes ago. I had a dream and would make it come true, no matter what.

The bus pulled in at a bus station near a restaurant so the passengers could use the washroom and grab a meal.

I opened the zipper of my handbag to get some belongings but decided it was safer to take my handbag with me and rushed to the restroom with one eye on the bus to ensure it didn't leave without me. That would be my biggest nightmare if it did. Quickly, I got back on the bus to devour the homemade sandwiches mom had packed for me. I groaned at the amazing taste.

No one could cook like my mother.

Late at night, after a fourteen-hour bus ride from Shiraz, the bus finally pulled into the Tehran bus terminal. I looked out the window, and happiness flooded me. I was finally in the center of Iran. Tehran was basically like the New York City of Iran.

The underpass of the terminal was dark and spooky. My heart started to flutter again when the realization hit that I was the only teenage girl traveling alone in a bus full of older men and women who belonged to those men. I couldn't help but feel like I was doing something wrong again.

I wondered, *If my dad was alive or if I had a brother of my own, would they ever let me embark on this journey?* They would be far stricter than my mom and would definitely prove to be a far more significant obstacle in this path I have chosen for myself.

My heart was fluttering in my chest. I had never traveled anywhere alone, and yet here I was. I felt like a lioness. A sense of pride and respect resurfaced for me. I collected myself again. There was still a long journey to cover. I didn't want my cockiness to get in my way. I looked ahead with confidence.

The passengers started getting off the bus one by one, carrying their belongings. Stepping off the bus meant losing the safety and cocoon I'd felt on board. I gathered my belongings, Big Brown, and exited the bus. The hustle and bustle of Tehran awaited me. I didn't have time for fear or jitters.

Tehran was like a giant maze. It was easy to get lost there. It was one of the places I always dreamed of visiting as a child. I couldn't believe I was standing on the soil of the capital city. Tehran was known for its vibrant colors, culture, and traditions. My mind kept reminding me that I was the only girl in my family and the only girl among my school friends who had traveled all the way from Shiraz to Tehran alone.

It was dark by the time we all got off the bus. The bus station seemed empty except for the fellow passengers. My eyes wandered around. The station seemed unresponsive and cold. I started to feel homesick, even though I had just landed there. I missed my mom and her warm embrace.

I worried about finding my way to Cousin Lily's house. Swiftly, I made my way to the nearby city bus stop. A few men were waiting at the dimly lit stop. Cautiously, I approached one man with a long, dark coat and a big mustache.

"Sir, could you please show me which bus to take to Abadi Street?" I asked him, keeping my voice as low as possible so it wouldn't attract any unnecessary attraction.

He raised his bushy eyebrows and looked at me from the corners of his eyes. He stared at me for a while before speaking.

"Where do you want to go, girl?" he asked in a grumbly, deep voice.

"Abadi Street; that's where my cousin lives, sir," I explained, so he wouldn't look at me suspiciously.

"Aha. Take bus number three. It will take you straight to Abadi Street, but be careful; this time of the night, a girl your age shouldn't be left alone. It's not safe," he commented.

Well, at least he looked sincere. I nodded. "Yes, sir, thank you."

I stood at the far corner of the bus stop and waited for bus number three. I started regretting my decision again. I didn't know why I was feeling like this again and again. These waves of discomfort kept sweeping me away. *How can I travel all the way to the USA alone?*

After a half-hour wait, bus number three finally arrived. Hefting Big Brown, I got on the bus with my eyes wide open. My eyes darted out for street names and traced them back to the map in my hands. There were only two other men on the bus aside from the driver. Thoughts of being alone with the three men on the bus were petrifying. I kept looking over my shoulder. I started praying for the safety of my life.

The bus driver finally called for Abadi Street passengers after what felt like an hour of driving. Happy to get another step closer to Lily's house, I got off the bus. I had never been to Lily's place before; I would be seeing her after so many years. Map and address in one hand, I dragged Big Brown with the other. I was exhausted from the journey.

The giant, white, dusty-looking board said *Abadi Street* with an arrow pointing toward the narrow alleyway. My hands turned clammy while I was holding my suitcase as I walked alone toward the dark alleyway at night. My grasp on Big Brown tightened as I swallowed a big lump.

Every step I took made noise; that was the only noise I could hear for kilometers. I took long strides to avoid getting kidnapped or worse. I swept a hand across my forehead to get rid of all the sweat. The streetlight was broken, but someone had deliberately tried to damage it. Which only indicated one thing. The aftermath of revolution. Young men would throw rocks at the streetlights to use the darkness to avoid being chased by the soldiers and the guards.

I shook my head with disappointment. Damaging your country's property was the height of cowardice in my eyes. It was hard to see the numbers on the houses in the dark.

"Number eleven, yes, this is it!" I exclaimed with relief. I had finally made it to Cousin Lily's place. It was past midnight, but Lily must have been waiting for me.

"Where have you been, girl? I was worried about you! How are you?" Lily exclaimed as soon as she opened the door.

"Hungry and tired," I said. The delicious aroma of food traveled to my nose.

"Come here, hug me, and have something to eat!" she said before embracing me.

I had never tasted such a delicious and hearty *Gormeh sabzi* stew and saffron rice. It could be because I was famished, but it was just beyond appetizing. It was a perfect combination of herbs and lamb with fluffy saffron rice on the side—just perfection.

After dinner, Lily and I chatted a bit. I enlightened her about my dreams and why I had come there. Although she was my cousin from my father's side, her loving nature reminded me so much of my mom. Lily had a darker complexion like my father. Her long, dark hair with few strands of gray was flowing over her shoulders. Her sweet smile reminded me of my dad. I felt safe and protected in her presence. Her home was beautiful, no doubt.

She noticed my exhaustion and showed me the warm and cozy bed she had prepared for me in her spare bedroom upstairs. I sank into the bed and fell into a deep slumber as soon as my face touched the cushiony pillow.

The following day, I woke up excited. All the exhaustion was no longer in my bones, and it was as if someone had taken all the weight off my shoulders. I glanced out the window.

The morning sun looked slightly different, so bright and welcoming as if it were trying to say, "It's a new day, Parvin. Seize the opportunity."

After freshening up and dressing, I came down to the kitchen. Lily's mouth-watering, flavorful omelet was ready on the table. I downed a bite of the omelet with a cup of tea and was ready to go out there and get the visa I had been dreaming of for a long time.

"Don't rush. Have another cup of tea and some more omelet. You have a long way ahead of you." She shoved a bite of omelet wrapped in flatbread in my mouth.

"Thank you, Lily. I have to go. I want to get there early."

My passport and university admission were tucked safely in my shoulder bag. I donned my *hijab* and headed out of her house.

"Time to go, Big Brown," I whispered.

Second Chance

> You can't go back and change the beginning, but you
> can start where you are and change the ending.
> —C. S. Lewis

A strange numbness settles within me as my attempt to get a visa yields no fruit. The word "hostage" rings inside my head again and again. It doesn't take long for my confusion to morph into denial. As I drag myself to Lily's place, the weight of defeat becomes unbearable with each step I take. The only sensible decision I made that day was to pack my bag and head back to Shiraz to my mom.

The prospect of showing my mother this defeat-filled face is another burdening task for me. At this point, I am a complete failure. All the hard work and my ability to juggle multiple jobs to save money to live out my dreams are going down the drain in front of me. I am feeling sick as my mind tries to comprehend this setback.

Maybe it was never meant to be. Perhaps Mom is right. This isn't the right path to choose. I have to get back home. Big Brown once held the power of wisdom, and her solace guided me, but she now appears to be just an ordinary bag. I feel like I could vomit right now and here. As I reach home, the first thing I do is lock myself in my room and cry.

Behind the door, I do not hear my mother calling for me. I settle on my hands and knees and let all my frustration out. I do not feel like talking to anyone at this point. I don't want them to see the utter humiliation and shame etched on every pore of my face, but most importantly, I do not want that humiliation to reflect back at me in the form of pitiful words and condolences.

All the doubts I had earlier when I decided to leave my homeland are now back.

I wipe my tears and start to unpack my bag haphazardly. As I get my belongings out of my bag, an outburst of grief envelops me. The overwhelming feeling returns, so I bury my face in my pillow and stay in a fetal position for a while so the pain will subside.

The more time I spend in my own company, the more I realize how it's all been a vivid dream. My goals come crashing down. I hide under my blanket, hoping the world will cease to exist when I emerge. My mom, day after day, attempts to bring me back. I know how hard it must be for her to see her child withering in agony, but I cannot help it. She tries to lull me away with her cooking so I will be willing to return to how things were. I just don't feel like leaving this cocoon of sadness. As I marinate in my sorrow and utter dejection, I realize that grief is such a funny little thing. It renders you immobile for weeks to come; it renders you inept.

Days begin to blur as I succumb to this grief. I spend most of my days in my room, staring out from the window or at the ceiling aimlessly, thinking about all the possibilities and options if the revolution hadn't happened. I linger on my bed and eat little food even though my mother tries hard to woo me with her tasty dishes.

I overthink all the trials and admonishments I endured to reach this point. The discrimination, the century-old traditions, the jobs I did, the warnings I have received over this short period—it was all for nothing. Another wave of misery washes over me, leaving my eyes puffy and sore from bawling like a baby.

No mother likes to see their child like this, so she tries her best to shield me from this anguish. She tries to lift my spirits, but no matter how much my family tries, there is no going back. Even then, I admire my mom's honest attempts to cheer me up.

How does one escape from such a profound setback? The road ahead of me that once held promises of liberty now looks void, full of darkness.

I begin to neglect myself. I avoid taking part in any household chores and basic self-care regimen. I cling to how I can make it through the day without being miserable. When I leave my house, I am bombarded with the unsettling gazes of people around me, as if they are mocking me or rejoicing in my defeat. The women in my neighborhood already found the idea of a girl traveling alone blasphemous, which explains why they look so satisfied. I look at my mom and see the weight of unspoken sorrow in her eyes. She might have been against my decision initially, but I am aware that a little part of her still wants me to succeed. Now, she can only offer a fleeting attempt at happiness for my sake.

Months pass, and with each ticking moment, the pressure intensifies. Life loses its meaning as the revolution robs me of all hopes and dreams. My mother tries to console me in her persistent efforts, yet the unyielding sadness within refuses to leave me.

Living becomes a mere façade; my aspirations are crushed. Sleep evades the painful reality. My heart aches at the realization that my dreams are now unattainable. Unsatisfied and overwhelmed with sadness, my days become monotonous. The dreams of freedom that once fueled my spirit now lie buried.

I watch Big Brown in the corner as she tries to offer her condolences.

In the depths of despair, I find myself in a mental abyss. I realize that I have now hit rock bottom. Amid these feelings, I decide to rejoin the dental office and resume work there because I already feel like a loser. I also do not want to feel like a burden to my mother.

One afternoon, lost in my thoughts, I ponder what my next steps in life should be. What should I do now? I walk down the street accompanied by my own bewildered musing. That's when I hear a voice as if someone is calling me from afar. It is faint, but it is certainly getting closer. I am startled by someone calling my name. Anxiously, I turn around and find my cousin Mahdy heading my way.

"*Salam*, Parvin," he greets me in his low voice. I am still processing his presence.

"Mahdy, what a surprise! What brings you here?" I ask. The last time I heard from him was via the letters we exchanged.

"Just passing by the old neighborhood. It is really good to see you, Parvin. How have you been?" he explains, his presence offering a glimmer of unexpected hope for some reason. We exchange words and greetings. I can tell he's analyzing my state. That's why he asked me this question. He can sense that I am not doing well.

"I am OK." I resort to a short answer, and he doesn't pry.

"How did it go with your American embassy? Did you get a visa?" Mahdy inquires, his concern evident, but his eyes are hopeful.

I am fearful of that exact question, but I reply with a heavy sigh.

"Didn't go well," I say, recounting the harrowing events of the hostage situation. As I unfold what had happened, I tell him about my journey to Tehran. Mahdy listens carefully and begins to comprehend the depth of my despair.

Mid-conversation, as I tell him everything from the start, I find my eyes getting watery again as residual emotions hit me like a truck. Tears spill down my face as I lay down all the grief that I have been holding together for weeks and months. I see Mahdy looking at me with sympathetic eyes; at least he doesn't have those condescendingly pitiful eyes others are offering me. I ramble in front of him. I struggle to convey the shards of my shattered dreams, but with each pressing second, as I lay my situation before him, I start to feel cathartic.

"I am so sorry, Parvin. Do not lose hope. There will be better things in store for you," he murmurs sympathetically. Then his eyes widen. "You really want to leave, don't you?"

"Yes, desperately," I say.

"Well, one of my former students when I used to teach English," he began, "his name is Safdar, and he's gone to India to continue his studies. We always exchange letters to keep in touch. He's been asking if anyone wants to come to India. He can help them. Would you like to go to India?"

I feel my body regaining energy again. Everything about my demeanor takes a shift upon hearing that offer. I start to tremble with excitement.

"Oh, wow, is that possible? Mahdy, I would love to."

I know I am expressing too much joy, but he has to understand how dire the situation is for me. This could be my only hope. I tell him about my studies and how I want to continue my education and enroll in a prestigious university.

I see great admiration and happiness in his eyes when I accept his offer. He has always supported my dreams, but since he is just my cousin, he has no right or permission to override my family and escort me out of Iran or take me anywhere.

"That settles it then. Don't worry, Parvin. I will connect you to Safdar."

My grief-filled days finally begin to dissipate as I long for a new dream. There is a slight change in plans. *India, here I come,* I tell myself. Thankfully, I am not alone in my desire to leave this country. Many like me yearn for freedom, so a man of his words, Mahdy connects me with Safdar.

I met Fadie and Sara when I was taking typing classes. Like me, they want to pursue further education abroad too. We became friends in a short span of time. We discuss our plan. I tell them what I want to do. We share ambitions. We map out our journey and question the feasibility of traveling to India in our circumstances.

Determined, we pack our bags and set course for Tehran, needing a place to stay. Fortunately, an older relative graciously welcomes us into her home. I am thankful for her thoughtful gesture.

On a bright afternoon, we are enjoying a cup of tea in her living room. Suddenly, she sits beside me and breaks the melodious silence.

"Why do you want to leave Iran anyway?" she asks our group innocently as she slurps her tea with us.

At this particular moment, a debate bubbles within. There are so many ways I can counter this question, but I am still contemplating how to respond because *what is not wrong with Iran these days?*

Yet, I hold my tongue, avoiding any quarrel or potential disturbance. We are her guests. I don't want to be rude to her—that's not how my mother raised me. Before I can utter a word, her eyes wander to me particularly. I am aware of the scrutiny in her eyes; growing up in the culture, I have gotten quite used to the look she is giving me now. She is about to launch a barrage of admonishments my way.

"You think you are doing the right thing educating and leaving your own country? You should be ashamed of yourself. How could you even think of leaving your mother alone?" she says all in one breath.

I put the cup down. Her words strike a chord, revealing a tender wound in my heart. I feel the weight of embarrassment. Her voice is shaking. I don't know how to process it. Discouragement engulfs me entirely. The hope and aspiration my cousin Mahdy instilled in me clashes with her stance.

She looks at me in resentment as if she happens to be my custodian, who is highly disappointed in me. Self-doubt creeps in on my plan. Yet again, I become a victim of my own overthinking.

I wonder, *What if she's right? Am I making the right choice? What am I even doing with my life?*

The stay at her house is far from pleasant. My friends and I stay only a little while. I promise myself not to return to her doorstep ever again. We head straight toward the Indian embassy, where we submitted all our documents earlier. Now, we eagerly wait for the outcome.

However, the passport isn't ready, and we don't know the reason for the delay, but it doesn't sound like good news to me. All of a sudden, another wave of remorse hits me. My relatives' venomous words haunt me. After a long wait in a cafe, we revisit the Indian embassy, and voila, our passports are finally ready, stamped with student visas.

My heart fills with joy. I feel a new kind of hope resurfacing. All these days passed in conflict and utter grief. This stamp on my passport holds so much promise. I am finally happy, but guilt still lingers in my silence. I get on the bus, and we embark on a fourteen-hour journey back to Shiraz. Slowly, as the bus approaches Shiraz, my happiness morphs into something else; I think about my mother. My friends are busy discussing all the places we'll visit in India and all the street food we'll try there; their enthusiasm is quite a boost, but my guilt tempers all my zest while thinking about how my mom will take this.

How could you leave your mother all alone?

I return home. I grapple with all the conflicting emotions in me. I want to escape this country. If India is a way to fulfill this decision, so be it. That was my ideal approach, but now I am vacillating. A lingering sense of regret stands against me like a mountain.

I manage to show my passport to my mother with a proud smile. *She has seen me grief-stricken, so she understands,* I thought. She looks at me with a small smile of contentment and nods. I know she's holding her words back, but I don't question her further.

The amount of sadness returns in the days leading to my departure, and only a few days remain until my flight. I keep looking at my mother. Although she is not mad at me, I see how she restrains herself. I cannot leave her like this.

I make up my mind right away and call my friends to return my ticket. I sink back into depression, feeling stuck and uncertain about my future.

Here I am, back where I started.

I am unable to free myself from this inner torment. The days turn into weeks and weeks into months, but I remain a lifeless soul trapped inside a country that thrives on breaking the souls of women down to ashes, but I don't see an immediate way out—I tried multiple times to get my wings and fly away, but one thing or the other always stopped me. Now, I have remained here willingly, desperately wanting to run away, but I can't. As the truth remains, I can't leave my mother alone in this country. However, the misery doesn't last long.

As I lay in bed one day, reluctant to confront the world, a ray of sunlight penetrates through my bedroom window, warming my entire being and casting a ray of hope upon my world. I sense a sudden change within me—a renewed zest for life. I'm unsure of the source of this sudden surge of hopefulness, but a wave of energy courses through me. The sun bathes the room in light, prompting me to reconsider my decisions. Realizing that action is necessary, I leap out of bed with newfound determination and let out a triumphant shout.

"*Māmān*, I have to go. I can't stay here." I pack my bag and take Big Brown with me, but first, I need to return to Tehran and renew my visa, as my old one has expired. My mother looks at me in complete shock as I pack in a frantic state.

"So, you are sure about this?" she asks, hooked to the doorframe with her arms crossed and tucked to her chest.

"Yes," I say. I insist on going and am not willing to change my decision yet again.

Seeing my determination, she acknowledges that she can't convince me otherwise. In fact, she offers something truly remarkable.

"Will it be OK if I come too?" she asks with a confused expression on her face. My joy doubles after hearing those words.

"Oh my God, *Māmān*, of course you can." I run toward her for a hug.

I am filled with overwhelming joy when I see support in her eyes. Despite her reservations about me leaving the country, I can see a mix of pride hidden somewhere behind all the stress and anxiousness, and that is all I need. We even have a conversation where she expresses her concerns about India and how I'll be able to manage, but it only deepens our bond.

9

Choices

Choices are the hinges of destiny.
—EDWIN MARKHAM

Beneath the veil of azure sky, my struggle in the search for freedom begins again. The breeze of liberty navigates my path to India as I travel for hours by bus, all the way from Shiraz to Tehran. The journey is about fourteen hours, but this time, I have my mother beside me—the guilt of disregarding her wishes suppressed by the serenity of her presence.

Arriving in Tehran, we navigate toward my cousin Lily's house and make ourselves at home there. Lily is a fantastic host. She's a gregarious personality brimming with love and kindness. She welcomes us with open arms and heart, instilling a tinge of comfort in our tired selves.

The flashbacks of my previous visit flicker before my eyes, as I had traveled an hour and a half from her place to the American embassy, but my mom's presence has shrouded the emotions of conflict and guilt this time. Warmth ripples through my soul, as I feel safe walking in her shadow because it means I have her approval. With a joyful smile playing on my face, we arrive at the embassy. Following the protocol, a spark of excitement ignites in my heart as I hand over my passport and university admission papers, knowing it is real this time.

My mind is already journeying through the streets of India as the specks of doubt disperse, and the decision—the vision of my departure—becomes more resolute, more vivid. While processing my documents, the front desk officer tells me to return in a couple of weeks to collect my passport with the possibility of a visa stamped on it.

I might finally go to the place where I can be free at last. Venturing out of the embassy, my mother and I stroll around the neighborhood, shopping for a raincoat that is recommended to take along to India due to heavy rainfalls in winter and spring. Momentarily, we take breaks in our stroll since my mother gets tired pretty quickly. We settle ourselves on the benches by the sidewalk. While my mother rests, I gaze at the sky, breathing the air that swirls, which is now perfumed by the essence of my dream.

In the state of trance, my mind wanders into the fragments of memories: my struggle, my thoughts of embarking on a new chapter of my life—one that is not tainted by the sense of imprisonment. I relish the thoughts of how I was an excited teen, brimming with boundless streams of energy to explore the world beyond the horizons of Iran. My thoughts powered my feet to embark on this journey, since no one I knew had tried to motivate me. The flare of inspiration burns brightly, ignited by the dexterity of my imagination, with which I had learned in times of turmoil and despair to shield and uplift myself.

The roots of fear sprout within me, as I have no clue about what I'm going to do or what to expect in this journey. I took every step I had to take, thriving on the urge and desire to breathe in the air of freedom, the thought of which became my motivation—my shield from the emerging fear—and drove me to overcome every obstacle in my path.

After shopping and bidding farewell to Cousin Lily, my mother and I return to Shiraz. A sense of success mixed with a tinge of anxiety swirls through me as I look forward to the day when I will receive my visa. A faint whisper of prayers lingers in the air as I peer at my mother beside me—she is chanting the prayers for the best outcome and for my protection. The melody of her whispering prayers blankets the warring emotions in my heart and infuses a sense of serenity and comfort in my soul. I rest back on the seat, hypnotized by her lullaby of prayers, knowing I have her backing and protection.

The sun paints the sky in its glorious aura as we arrive back in Shiraz the next day, and I book my flight to Hyderabad. The last time I had booked my tickets, I was with my friends, Fadie and Sara, who were leading. This time, I am all alone and have to be my own guide as I figure out the ways of the world. After conducting some research, I find a travel agency. We don't have a telephone line at home, so everything has to be done in person to gain further insight into the matters at hand.

Along with every step, the roots of fear tangle my feet—the fear of the unknown. Gulping the pill of courage, I tread forward.

I decide that there is no room for fear and that I will not let my dreams vanish again because of them. I blink away my fears as if they are a nagging, dull pain. The thoughts of flying in the skies by plane spark a tinge of excitement within me, while embers of fright burn faintly too. The gate into the realm of dreams is close; I can see it, and nothing can stop me from opening it this time.

The tickets I bought for Hyderabad, India, cost me a significant amount of the money I had saved from working at the dental office. Pouring the emotions of ecstasy into my words, I write a letter to Fadie and Sara and ask them to pick me up from Hyderabad Airport. Since I am aware of my lack of knowledge of languages besides *Farsi*, I realize I can't do anything without their help.

As the days dwindle away, I pack my belongings in my big, brown suitcase again. Disbelief still lingers within my mother and is triggered as she sees me preparing for my trip again.

"I was hoping you would give up on leaving," her voice echoes as I notice her standing at the living room door, peering at me with a hint of sadness flickering in her eyes.

"No, *Māmān*. I have to leave, and now is the time," I reply, embedding my resolve in my words.

A deep sigh escapes her mouth, accompanied by a slight poof between her lips. The grief and worry shadow her eyes as I can see it vividly swirling in there.

"Don't worry. I'll be all right, and it might not even happen. I might not even get the visa," I console her with a wavering smile, as I can't bear the sadness on her face. She glances at me and aims her gaze toward the ceiling as if she is looking past it and murmurs.

"God, tell me what to do. I don't know anymore," she prays in a defeated voice and strides out of the room. The fog of guilt and sadness lingers over my soul, seeing the desperation in my mother's heart.

Hurrying through the days, filled with anticipation and a torrent of emotion, finally, the day to pick up my passport from the Indian embassy arrives. The fear suffocates my excited heart as the thought of not getting the visa envelops my mind. Carving myself out of the dome of fear, I plan the whole scenario of events in my mind. *I'll go to Tehran to see if my visa is ready, in which case, I'll leave. Otherwise, I will return to Shiraz.*

As I wander through these scenarios, a shiver spirals down my spine. I find myself entangled between the two choices—both of them frightening in their own aspect. Tearing myself away from my past, my present—my home—and settling in a new country makes my heart quiver, but staying put in this country means submitting my soul to living a lifeless life, a life of a puppet being controlled by her family, husband, society, and the government. Weighing both of these scenarios gives me enough motivation to help me push forward through the shackles of fear and liberate myself from the control of immediate emotions.

Seeing the flickers of sadness in my mother's eyes and hearing her words makes my resolve tremble, but I am pumped up, eager to move on from the suffocation I feel in this country, and there is no way she can change my mind. Ultimately, seeing the fire of passion burning brightly in my eyes, she finally accepts that I have made my decision and nothing can change my mind.

However, I know the reality of my emotions—I am terrified. Still, the reward of breathing the air of freedom is so vital to me that it shields my decision and blocks out anything and everything that will hinder my resolve and stop me from moving forward. To mitigate the stress, I break down the long journey into little steps: the first stop is Tehran, and there is nothing after that. Second, when I reach Tehran, my only goal will be to reach Cousin Lily's place. The rest will follow. Keeping my focus on the immediate steps before me, I am now holding the reigns over my emotions.

The moment of truth is here; I say goodbye to my sisters and their families. My protective shield shatters into fragments; my heart is broken, but I gulp back my tears. Leaving my sisters and my little nieces and nephews behind is not easy. It eats away at my core, but I put on a mask of confidence so I won't cause them any more grief. After all, it is my decision to leave, and I should shoulder the weight of the pain of separating from them.

My mother decides to accompany me to the bus terminal. Walking in her presence, I feel protected, but part of me knows that saying goodbye to her will rip my soul apart. Waiting at the bus terminal, enveloped in the cold, brisk breeze of December and embraced by the sunlight, my mind strolls into past events.

Around the same time before, I traveled to Tehran for my US visa, but the events at the American embassy and their hostage-taking drove me to suffer the effects of trauma, and the path to my dreams crumbled. My heart prays repeatedly, never to experience that again. As the gate to the realm of dreams nears, I grow impatient, praying that nothing will crush it this time.

Sitting on the bench beside my mom, blessed by the sun's warmth, my gaze quenches its thirst as it roams around the surroundings. I can't take my eyes away from everyone and everything around me, as I think it might be the last time I get to see my city—my people. Soon, the bus arrives, and my mother helps me load my big, brown suitcase into the storage compartment under the bus.

"Passengers going to Tehran! All aboard!" the driver yells from his seat.

The moment has arrived—the moment to say goodbye to my mother. I stare into my mom's eyes, upwelling tears, and my heart sinks into the pools of guilt and sadness as I give her a big hug. Tears trickle down her beautiful face. Everything I went through in this process—every sorrow and trial I faced—all seem insignificant in the face of this. Nothing can fill my essence and soul more with sorrow than seeing those beads of pain and helplessness roll down my mother's cheeks. Under the overwhelming emotions at that moment, I choke, utilizing every bit of my energy to hold back my tears.

"I might be back. I might not even get the visa, so don't be sad, *Māmān*. I love you," I whisper the words of consolation in her ears, holding back my own whimpers as I try to comfort her.

I get on the bus; my head turns, and my gaze fixes on her face—a canvas of sorrows and pain. Once on and settled in my seat, I locate my mother from the bus window; she is still waiting there, her eyes roving around, trying to find me on the bus. Equipping myself with a painful smile, I wave at her and send her kisses as I scream from the bus window, "I will be all right, *Māmān*, don't worry!"

Soon, the bus drives off, and the image of my mother grows further away with each blink until she fades into the distance and disappears as the bus turns toward the highway. The emotions that I had reined in now rage violently in me as the thoughts of guilt manipulate my mind.

Am I being selfish? Should I give up what I want to make my family happy?

The guilt slowly eats away at my heart, tearing at it minute after minute. Fate gave me two destinies—both filled with their distinctive trials and tribulations.

I know the road ahead won't be easy if I leave for India. The path forward is difficult to travel; I must walk on thorns to achieve my dream of freedom.

I worked so passionately and hard to get to where I am, I say to myself.

On the flip side, staying at home and settling down means misery for the rest of my life—a life where I will never be able to see even a glimpse of freedom. The thoughts of staying back home suffocate my mind as if I am imprisoned even in my thoughts, but staying back will make my family happy. I am drowning in the narrow streams of my choices as these thoughts flood my brain.

As I soar through these overwhelming thoughts, I decide that I will not allow others' expectations of me to stop me from pursuing and attaining what I believe is best for me. The urge to leave the country shines brightly within me, dispersing the creeping emotions and transforming my will into a mighty one—a strong nineteen-year-old girl embarking on her unstoppable mission.

Enduring the fourteen-hour-long journey, I arrive again at Cousin Lily's house in Tehran. The next day is the day of reckoning: when I am supposed to pick up my Indian visa. The blanket of a starry night shrouds the skies as I toss and turn in my bed all night, unable to sleep from the uncontrollable excitement. Tired but determined, I make my way to the Indian embassy and soon find myself holding this treasured passport to freedom. I am one more step closer to my dream manifesting into a reality.

The sun of dreams rises from the eastern horizon, imbuing the sky in golden hues, as I can actually smell my freedom for the first time on the breeze. The unnerving time to take the final step is in front of me. The battle between fear and courage, self-sabotage and self-care, and love and hate escalate in me—an internal war that I have never experienced to this level before. I crave the safety of home, my mother's serene presence. The taste of a cup of warm soup passed to me by her hands lingers on my tongue; my eyes long for her affectionate gaze. The joyful conversations with my sisters and the playfulness of my nieces and nephews flicker through my mind—a dream that I have just woken up from.

Manipulated by the turmoil of emotions inside me, I turn to Cousin Lily for emotional support as tears of homesickness swell up in my eyes.

"Girl, why do you want to go? Stay here with your family where it's safe. Don't go," she replies as a tinge of worry reflects in her eyes, but it seems like she is now on my family's side too. In this moment, the only ray of hope of support fades away. The fear digs deeper into my soul, and I quietly pull myself away from her.

Why can't they just support me?

The thought swarms my mind. Everyone seems to know me better than I do. The quality of trust in the threads of bond between us seems nonexistent as they question my abilities in every decision I make for myself. The specks of hatred erupt in my heart because no one can believe in me.

My mind drills into the world of wishful thinking as I think, *If only I were a boy, maybe my family could then trust that I can take care of myself.*

The faint echoes of my mom's voice reverberate in my mind, telling me that girls are not made to take big steps like this. *Stay back with your family where it's safe.*

The hopes of contact with my family vanish into thin air as Cousin Lily and my mother don't have any telephone lines. All my responsibilities are now on my own shoulders, an experience I have never known before. This is something I have wished for my entire life. As much as I despise people making decisions for me, in reality, my family and the social circle around me dictate most of my life. I despise this cycle, but I noticed most women around me don't even notice that decisions are being made for them—the rules are accepted without any question.

This revolution inside me; this sudden change makes me realize that shouldering the burdens of my life and weighing the decisions before making them will not be easy. I realize the battle is inside me. It is time to commit to trusting myself, something others have failed to do. Whether to make the right decisions in life or let others dictate my life for me, the choices before me are clear. Committing to that trust in myself means I have to walk into an unknown future where the path will either be filled with trials or peace. Either way, only I will be responsible for my actions and have control over my life.

On the other hand, staying back means being forced to marry a guy I barely know and start a family with him, and when things become intolerable, and my life turns miserable, I can lay the blame on others, but it won't make any difference. I will be stuck in that chasm of blame and misery.

My choice now is clear—thoughts of being stuck, unable to do anything, that choice is out of the question now. That lifestyle isn't for me. I want to have power over my life; delegating control and blaming others means taking that power away from myself and handing the reigns of my life to others. I know I am not ready to do that.

The next few days at Lily's are nerve-racking for me—filled with turmoil, yet some of the most awakening days of my life. The thought of being in a strange country without any knowledge of the culture or language makes me anxious. Aside from my mother tongue, *Farsi*, I don't know any other languages. My linguistic competency in English is limited to just a few phrases and words I learned as a second language in high school. This is tangled between anxious thoughts like, *What if Fadie and Sara don't show up to pick me up from Hyderabad Airport?*

I drown in a pool of distress.

The fear of not having any support in a foreign country strangles my soul, and the thoughts of missing my nephews and nieces feel like sizzling lava being poured onto my head, but I hold onto the rope of trust in myself that secures me, and I decide to be strong and strengthen my will to be a wise decision-maker for my own sake.

Things would've been so much easier if I had someone's support and someone to rely on if I stumbled along the path. In the realm of wishful thinking, I think, *Who else but God will be the best support I could get?* With that, I decide to do something I have never done before, the very thing I always teased my mom about.

I confer with Lily to ask that we go to the *mullah* at the local mosque to read my fortune and tell me whether I should go to India or not. The way it works is, in the Shia Muslim tradition, each page of the holy book of the Qur'an has *good*, *neutral*, or *bad* written at the top of the page. If you have a decision to make and you are having a hard time deciding, you ask the holy book for guidance. You hold the closed Qur'an in one hand and shut your eyes, peer into your heart, and then ask your question, while with the other hand, you open a page of the Qur'an. Looking at what is written on top of the page will provide your answer: good, neutral, or bad.

So, we follow the procedure, and I ask whether I should go to India and open my eyes, my core dwindling in mixed emotions as *mullah* reads my fortune and the page I had chosen has written *Bad* on the top.

My expectations drop into hopelessness as I think, *Does this mean I have to go back to Shiraz and forget about my hopes, dreams, and all the effort I had to put in to get here?*

My trust in myself breaks as I burst into tears. Lily embraces me in her arms and tries to instill comfort in my wailing heart as she says, "Qur'an says you shouldn't go, child. Maybe you should go back to your family."

The demons of loneliness haunt my heart as only one thought swirls in my mind at that moment. *I can't even get God's support in this. I truly am alone in this journey.*

Once again, I weigh the choices I have. Marching back to the life I want to leave behind means being shrouded in a full-covering *chador* and obeying the fundamentalist rules Ayatollah has enforced upon the people of Iran. It means accepting that I am not as good as a man. It means I have to live with being treated like a slave to men and handing over the reins of my life to them.

If I go back, I will feel I have failed myself for the rest of my life.

I have to decide; time is not my friend on this journey. My flight is in two days, and I must decide the course of my life at that moment. I choose not to bend in front of the dictatorship, not to be shackled by their beliefs of how I should be living; accepting this will be accepting that my soul and dreams are to be wrapped in chains and tossed into an abyss, never to sense freedom again.

I opt to ignore everyone's disagreement; no one can stop me if it means living my life in the graces of freedom.

Ultimately, I dismiss the *mullah*'s fortune-telling and regain my confidence. The decision that shackled my mind before became clear and finalized for me. I close my heart, shielding it from all the negative emotions. I bask in self-support, which gives me the strength and courage to move forward. I feel a strong force is behind my decision, helping me see things clearly. I know my path will be filled with obstacles, but confidence is again brimming within me, and I know I can resolve them.

Successful, independent people have always illuminated my heart with the light of inspiration. People who created a more fulfilling life, tackling the trials of their chosen life rather than accepting an ordinary one.

If my friends Fadie and Sara could do it, so can I, I remind myself, pouring confidence into my soul. The only difference is that their families were emotionally and financially supportive of their decision, and they didn't have to jump through as many hoops as I did.

It doesn't matter. I have been able to do it all by myself so far, and I can manage the rest of my journey by myself. I strengthen my will as I say these words of confidence to myself.

Cousin Lily is surprised when I reveal to her my decision to go to India after all.

"You mean you are going to dismiss *mullah*'s fortune-telling?" she protests, a hint of surprise lingering in her voice.

"Yes, Lily," I answer with an apologetic gesture. I can see the emotions of shock, worry, and sadness swirling in her by the way her jaw drops and her eyebrows knit together.

"Well, child, I said what I had to say," she exclaims. Then she continues, "But maybe you should talk to your family first."

I take a moment to ponder over what she said, but I think talking to my mom about this again will be useless. I know in my heart that this time around, no matter what they say, my decision won't change, so I keep quiet. If I talk to my family, they will try to talk me out of it. Now, nothing can stop me from attaining the freedom I always wanted.

To prepare myself to march into a new chapter of my life, I visit the nearby bazaar the same day and buy myself a fake engagement ring. This way, I ensure that no man will try to approach me if they see I am already engaged. The ring is a protective amulet against the trauma of being harassed by men.

No man can stop me from living the life I want now, I say to myself.

With the ring on my finger, I am all set and prepared to walk on the path I chose for myself.

Leaping Beyond the Edge

The hero is no braver than the ordinary man,
but he is brave five minutes longer.
—RALPH WALDO EMERSON

The cold winds of December gust through the house as I lay awake through the night. The anxiety and the stress of the unknown are drowning my consciousness as today is the day I embark on my journey to India. Today, the sun of reckoning rises from the eastern horizon, its luminous rays illuminating my soul with a spark of hope. Veiling the whirlpool of emotions inside me, taking a shower, wiping away the splotches of stress from my soul, and shrouding myself in the dress for my journey, I stroll downstairs.

The aroma of the eggs and herbs makes my stomach growl. Marching downstairs with my appetite growing, I see Cousin Lily preparing the traditional breakfast for me and my big, brown suitcase already sitting in the doorway. My eyes fail to avert from Cousin Lily. Complex emotions swirl within me as I think, *This may be the last time I see her.* A tinge of sadness crosses my heart, but now is not the time to be sad. I have to be strong. This is the journey I have dreamt of for a long time, and I can't let my resolve waver. The enchanting breakfast sits in front of me now, the oil still sizzling on top of the egg with a mix of herbs on top of feta cheese and dry fruit decorated in a bowl next to it.

I can feel my worries vanishing as I eat my way through it, each tastebud relishing the delicate taste of it. It's a breakfast that I can't forget no matter how much time passes; it is a memorable gift. I know the time to bid farewell to Cousin Lily will soon be upon me.

My anxiety begins to transform into an orb, capturing my heart and resolve within it. I have eaten so much, but Cousin Lily insists that I finish everything. I cannot take another bite, but it would be disrespectful if I deny it. I'm feeling nauseous as I consume everything on my plate, and then I notice her bringing a cup of tea for me.

"You have a long day ahead of you. You have to eat," Cousin Lily says. I drink from the hot cup of tea, and immediately, the burning sensation sends shivers through my tongue, but I know I can't refuse right now—after all, I can do this much for the person who is caring for me in her own way. My eyes refuse to leave the clock on the wall as I see time escaping gradually. This is my chance at freedom, and I can't let anything take it away from me. No matter how fearful I am, I'll push through.

The numbing sensation still lingers on my tongue, and my stomach cramped with breakfast. It's now time for me to take the next step in my journey. Wrapping my scarf around my head and pulling on my manteau, blanketing myself from head to toe, I am now ready.

The honk of the car echoes through the street—it is Cousin Lily's son, Hassan, waiting for me. A gust of emotions swirls through me as I peer back at Cousin Lily standing there with tears in her eyes. This is the last time I will see her. My heart steeps in the pits of sorrow as I gaze upon her sad face. Clenching my fists, I stride forward and hug her, absorbing her pain, her sorrows, in my embrace as I struggle to hold back my tears.

"Take care of yourself," words carrying the weight of pain in my heart escape my mouth in the form of a whisper.

I can feel her head nodding as her arms envelop me tighter and then let go of me. Flourishing a smile on my face, I veil the emotions of my thumping heart as I turn away and march outside. I can feel the warmth of the sun enveloping me, the cold, brisk breeze of December guiding my footsteps as I reinforce my resolve with the thought of Big Brown being at my side. Strolling forward, I hop in the car and greet Hassan as we drive off to the airport.

The faces of my family, whom I left behind, are flashing through my mind as the scenery around us blurs. I can tell that the shadow of my emotions engulfs my face in its darkness. Noticing the worries reflecting on my face, Hassan starts to chat about different subjects to carve my mind out of the thoughts of the airport and the flight. The journey is about an hour and a half to the Mehrabad airport, now known as Emam Khomeini Airport, after the revolution.

After traveling for more than an hour, we stand in front of the airport now. I have never visited an airport before, but the sight before me is marvelous—huge. My eyes wander around it, trying to capture its magnificence in them. It is finally happening. The sound of the crowd echoes through the building, with people rushing in and out of it with their loved ones.

It is a place where tears bid goodbye to the ones going abroad and smiles welcome the ones coming home.

I can feel the emotions resembling the state of my heart—sadness mixed with happiness. The thud of the big, brown suitcase carves me out of my trance as Hassan puts her down.

It is time for yet another farewell, and I want to hug and thank him for all he has done for me, but I can't. The rules and regulations imposed by the new government forbid women to touch men, even handshakes. Imbuing emotions of thankfulness in my eyes, I say goodbye to him as I carry Big Brown and navigate through the crowd. My soul chanted the cries of hope—hoping he understands the intensity of my gratefulness toward him and his family.

My eyes and heart dwell in disbelief as they capture the sight of bulletin boards, the TVs, the gadgets I had never seen in my life before. For some reason, I can't lift my steps. It feels like I have been frozen in the middle of the airport, not knowing what I'm supposed to do next.

I have never been to an airport, nor do I know any procedure. I stand there frozen with my tickets in my hand as claws of fear bury my feet into the ground. My mind warps into the memories of the time when my mother bought a thirty-two-inch black-and-white TV and placed it in my dad's room.

Since his death, I wouldn't bring myself to step inside that room as the emotions lingering in there have been too much for my wailing heart. I couldn't bring myself to submerge myself into his memories, but when my mother decided to put the new TV in my dad's old room, after a couple of weeks or so, I convinced myself to step into his room and begin watching television.

The remembrance of that moment sprouts courage in me—the courage to take the step, and everything will be fine after that. Remembering all the struggle I went through to arrive at this moment, I lift my feet, manifesting every bit of courage in me, and ask the people around for the next steps, like where I am supposed to go and such.

Some people provide me with directions and procedures. Taking their advice, I march toward the check-in area. Now that I have my boarding pass, I must let go of my luggage. I lift my big, brown suitcase, and put it on the belt. Slowly yet steadily, I witness it fading into the darkness of a hole, sprouting uncertainty within me. Clenching my fists, I tell myself that it's fine. I'll claim her back soon.

Puffing out the weight of my emotions, I walk toward another section and ask around about the details of the next procedure. They tell me to go through the security check in the women's area. The security woman searches about my body as I stand there motionless, my heart thumping wildly, hoping that nothing goes wrong.

After searching my body, she asks me about the little pouch hanging around my neck.

"What is this?" she asks as she holds it in her hand.

"My mom made me a little pouch so I can put money in there. I hung it around my neck so I won't lose it," I explain as I open the pouch and show her the hidden money. I have around four thousand German marks. Counting through the money, she allows me to keep it, as it isn't above the limit, and I am now another step closer to my flight to India.

Marching out of the security check room, I tread toward the guy sitting behind the desk.

"Are you going with your family?" he asks as he goes through my passport.

"No, I'm alone," I reply, hoping for all of it to be over soon.

Suddenly, he looks up with surprise flickering in his eyes, and I can see why he is surprised. It is odd for a woman to travel alone, but this is my destiny, and I have endured my share of those looks.

"Alone, huh? You have relatives there?"

"No, I'm going to study."

"Do you know their language?"

"No, I don't know any language besides *Farsi*," I respond, thinking maybe it is part of the process to provide them with answers.

"How are you going to do this alone? You are a pretty girl and engaged too. You should be staying home with your family," he starts to blabber the same things I listened to since I thought of this journey.

Part of my soul absorbs his words as the fog of worries begins to cloud my heart again. *Am I doing something wrong? What do I do?* I think as terror screams within my soul. Struggling through my fears, I arrive at the conclusion that it's too late to worry about such things—the dream I always dreamt of is in my grasp, and I will be strong no matter what. Taking my passport and tickets back from him, I march toward the waiting area and sit on the metal chairs.

Hours pass by as my eyes keep hovering through the hordes of people marching in and out, a tinge of numbness crawling through my spine. Their murmurs about the terminal and flight number fall on my ears, drowning me in the realm of thoughts, *What's a terminal? Flight number?*

I question myself as I have no idea what any of these things mean. As anxiousness boils inside me, I ask the people around me about these things, and they reveal to me that I'm supposed to wait in the waiting area until they announce my flight to Bombay.

"Passengers for Bombay, aboard," the announcer's voice reverberates through the hall.

It is my flight. The moment for which I have been struggling for a long time is now here. Manifesting courage in my heart, I march through the terminals and up the stairs to board the plane. As I stand on the top of the stairs, I wander my eyes around the airport. This is the last time I'm going to see this land, breathe this air, or see these people.

A rush of emotions envelopes me in its turmoil, and the orb of anxiety begins to throb in my heart once again. Fear surges through my veins with sadness and a tinge of happiness mixed in. Tears of complex emotions sparkle in my eyes; I avert my consciousness from the surroundings and stride inside the plane.

Suddenly, I find myself surrounded by all the gadgets and technology I have never seen before since it is my first time inside a plane. Astonishment surrounds my quivering heart as the stewardess guides me to my seat beside a window.

"Everyone, kindly buckle up your seatbelts, as we are about to take off," the captain's voice erupts from the speakers.

I find myself drowning in a torrent of emotions—mixed emotions of joy and sadness—as I peer out of the window, submerging the landscape of my homeland in my memories. Averting my eyes from the window, I grab the seatbelt and play with it for a while since I don't know how to buckle it up.

Nervousness arises within me, but the stewardess comes and helps me buckle up. She must have seen me struggle with it. A loud, revving sound drums through me as the land outside starts to get smaller and smaller, and after a while, eventually disappearing into the fog of clouds as we fly high up in the air. Momentarily, feelings of loneliness start to gush through me. I'm scared; my reality hits me suddenly as I crave the embrace of my mother, her protection.

Peeling off the look of worry from my eyes, I see another girl around my age sitting beside a mature woman who seems to be her mother on the seat beside me.

The woman's gaze pierces through me as she notices my nervousness vivid on my face and asks, "Where are you going?"

"I'm going to Hyderabad to study," I answer.

"Do you have anybody there?"

"I have a couple of friends. We are supposed to meet at the airport."

"Do you know the Indian language?"

"No, I don't."

During the bombardment of questions, she stares at me with a questioning yet surprised look.

"Wow! You are so daring. Like, you might get lost, or somebody might try to kidnap you, rob you, or take advantage of you because you don't know anything." She suddenly starts to fan the fears that thrived within me since the start of this journey.

Her words sink into my soul as I ponder my decision and what awaits me in a foreign land. The shackles of fear bind around my core tightly as my body starts to shiver. I can feel my heart pounding ferociously, clawing its way out of my chest. All the fears I had enclosed in the back of my consciousness are now crawling back out, holding the reigns of my mind. Her words opened the gates of traumatizing memory, which I had veiled in the deepest corners of my brain—the day I was almost kidnapped.

I was six years old when my dad gave me money and told me to buy some sugar from the store on the corner of the street. Being made responsible for the task of an elder, I felt proud as I marched to the store when a mature man called me and whispered to me, "Oh, little girl, come here. Can you help me?"

Being enticed by his request, by the thought that an elderly person needed my help, I went closer, and he showed me a piece of paper and a bag of chips in his other hand.

"Can you tell me if this address belongs to that house?" he asked as he pointed in a certain direction. I felt brimming with pride as I had just finished grade one, and I could read, but as we marched in that direction … it was a dead end in a dark alley.

"Can you check the house number?" he asked as he showed me the piece of paper, leaned in closer, and grabbed my hand. Even my six-year-old brain screamed something was wrong. Fear vibrated through me as I pulled myself away, and he pulled me toward himself. Struggling for a while, I pulled myself free as I fell to the ground and ran away. I picked up sugar from the store, my heart still pounding heavily as specks of fear painted my face.

When I went home, I explained the event that took place to my mother. I remembered her words: never to trust a strange man.

The remembrance of these memories drives my being into the abyss of sadness and fright. I begin to contemplate future events, like, what if I can't find my friends at the airport? If they don't, I'm screwed. The thoughts ravage through my mind as the woman's words swirl in my mind.

"Well, that's why I'm taking my daughter to India and making sure she has a place to live, she's well off, goes to university there, and she is safe to stay. Then I'll come back to Iran," she continues.

Sadness subdues my consciousness as I remember my mother, wishing that she would have been with me. Like this woman, she should have been protecting me. Tremors of fear ripple through my body as I don't know anything anymore; my existence gradually drowns into loneliness as I question my decisions. "What have I done?" I say to myself as the fear growls within me, enclosing my heart in its prison of sorrows.

After shivering in the coldness of fear, I think, *No! This is not the time for you to be afraid. Whatever lies in your path, you must face it and survive.*

105

I can feel my fears fading away slowly as these words sink into my soul. Sighing out the coldness of fear and emotions, I encourage myself that nothing is impossible. I have done it so far, and I can do the rest by myself.

"I'm not going to think about where I am right now. I'll think of the next step. That's it, I'm not going to scare myself with these thoughts," I say to myself as I empower my will with consolation and planning.

The land starts to near as we descend from the skies. After navigating through the crowd inside the plane, I march out the door as the piercing heat punches my face. Even in the midst of December, the intensity startles me as my body drenches with sweat, my scarf sticking to my skin. Suffocation starts to soar within my veiled body as I follow everyone into the terminal to ready myself for my next flight from Bombay to Hyderabad.

As I tread into the airport, the vibrance imbued in the canvas widens my eyes in awe. There are so many colors! Since the revolution, all the colors have been taken away from us except black, brown, and navy, even from men and children. Now, in this land of my dreams, women are wearing saris flourishing with a variety of vibrant colors—without any head covering. This is breathtakingly beautiful. Freedom is beautiful and colorful!

"Oh my God! This is how it used to be for us," I say to myself as my eyes glimmer with the colorful landscape and people before me.

My heart refuses to believe as it pounds excitedly, shedding the remnants of fear and sadness away. The aroma of spice, curry, and coconut oil lingers in the air as I breathe in the freedom, my soul rejuvenating in the liberating energy that swirls around me.

Some part of me feels scared, as this is a foreign country. As I march deeper into the airport, I see men wearing khaki shorts with funny hats that I had never seen before. Their chocolate-colored skin reveals the whites of their eyes like stars twinkling in the blanket of night. Suddenly, I feel nature's call to use the washroom as I break out of my trance and think about how I should ask someone for directions.

A tinge of fear arises as I instantly remember the flash cards my cousin helped me write—a compilation of the prominent sentences and phrases that could help me till I reach my friends. They were written in *Farsi* and translated into English.

Before wasting any moment, I take out my cards and show the people around me to help me navigate my way, and so begins my journey in the country of India.

The Angel in Blue

Every experience in your life is being orchestrated to
teach you something that you have chosen to learn.
—LOUISE HAY

Amid the murmurs of the crowd and the strange faces, I flit from one
person to another, holding my flashcard with *Where is WC?* written
on it (WC = water closet). I let my gaze wander around the airport,
looking for signs that might help me navigate my way, but I can find none. As
I revolve from person to person, one woman nearby seems safe and friendly.
I march toward her, revealing my flashcard to her.

She aims her gaze at me, peering into me as if I were some alien who can't
speak her tongue. Grasping onto the thread of hope, I stride toward another
woman, and this time, I read the contents of my card aloud but receive the
same reaction. "WC" is an acronym that I learned in high school English
class; I don't know, and I don't understand why they can't understand me.

As confusion and anxiousness cloud my mind, a lady in a vibrant-blue
sari, her long, dark, braided hair trailing behind her, approaches me. I figure
she has been watching me desperately hop from one person to another, for
directions.

"What are you looking for, girl?" she asks me in *Farsi*, imbued with an Indian accent.

Disbelief starts to swarm over me, as I'm not able to believe people speak *Farsi* here too. A tinge of excitement and relief swirls within me. I show her my flashcard and ask her for directions to the washroom. A gentle smile flourishes on her face, and her big, brown eyes light up as she asks me to follow her and navigates me through the colorful crowd and to the women's washroom.

"I will wait for you here. Leave your suitcase with me," she says.

Among the gratitude that flows through me for her help, specks of worry taint my mind. I just met her, so how can I trust her with my big, brown suitcase—my friend, my companion on this journey? Hastily, I march into the washroom. Fear of her vanishing with my suitcase lingers in me. At the same time, I don't want to lose grasp of my only thread of connection to this world since no one else in this foreign land understood my language.

I look into the mirror on the washroom wall before exiting. *You have the will to face the challenges and trials that lay ahead on your path to Hyderabad,* I murmur. At the same time, I pray that the woman in the blue sari wouldn't have escaped with Big Brown. As I exit the washroom, I lift my eyes and see that she is standing in that same spot with my suitcase beside her. Surprise and gratitude for her honesty consume my senses.

Radiating a smile of relief on my face, I grab my suitcase and drag it behind me as we chatter on our way back to the terminal.

"Where is your destination?" she asks in *Farsi*. I see a shine in her large, brown eyes when she hears Hyderabad.

"Oh, I am also going to Hyderabad."

Comfort finds its way into my troubled heart as she becomes my ray of hope in this foreign land, a helpful guardian.

As we chatter along our way, she discloses how she has lived in Iran for a few years and learned *Farsi* there. "It was a good life before the revolution, but now, it's another story. It's time for me to stay in India," she says.

I can feel my eyes sparkling with excitement, as if God has served the world to me on a silver platter. Ecstasy surges in my heart as the belief sprouts—the belief that I have found my savior. *I think I will call the lady in the blue sari my angel, for she is nothing less than that in my eyes.*

"Don't worry. Since we are both going to the same place, I'll show you the way to the flight going to Hyderabad. Just follow me," she consoles me as we both stride forward and search for our gate.

The angel in blue stays with me throughout the process of checking in at the gate and waiting to board. I feel safe to have her by my side. We board the plane. I locate and settle in my seat. The sight of the plane makes me realize that even though it's huge, it isn't as big as the one I boarded previously. As the passengers start to pour into the plane, I lose sight of my angel, but part of me feels comfortable, knowing that she is there.

As the flight takes off, I reevaluate my plan—my next step in this journey. This next step will be much easier compared to what I have faced so far because my friends, Fadie and Sara, will be there to pick me up from the airport.

As I get comfortable in my seat, the words of the woman from Tehran who sat beside me on my last flight resound in my head, shackling my excitement in the chains of worry and fear. Every time her words echo in my head, my stomach ties into knots, and beads of sweat erupt from my palms.

I have never been a religious person, but now I can't help but pray, "Dear God, help me find my friends. Dear God, don't let anyone rape me, and please, help me find my way." I feel guilty for praying out of desperation.

As the plane tears through the skies of Bombay, I glue myself to my seat, pouring every bit of energy into my arms as I hold onto the armrests of my seat and continue praying. In an attempt to divert my mind from the troubling thoughts, I remind myself of the list of things I need to be ready for when the plane lands.

I should remember my passport and my handbag, I think, as I'm not sure what else I should be expecting. Instantly, the thought of my companion—my big, brown suitcase—flashes through my mind as I wonder, *How will I get Big Brown back?* We separated at the terminal, where I assume they loaded her in the storage compartment of the plane.

After soaring through the skies for about an hour and a half, the plane finally lands in Hyderabad. I gather my belongings, following others' lead, and among the hoard of passengers, I tread down the stairs and out toward the terminal. As I stand at the top of the stairs, my footsteps come to a halt. I skim my hand over my scarf, shrouding my head since I left Iran. The sense of security still fails to envelop me as my heart shivers with fear, and I feel reluctant to remove my *hijab*.

As I walk into the terminal, the piercing, loud noises penetrate through me as I step into the airport. The architecture of the airport seems rundown, more like a degraded version of the Bombay airport. The familiar smell of coconut oil and spices swirls in the air, but this time, more intensely. The aroma of spices hallucinates my mind, making me feel like I was strolling around in somebody's kitchen—and brewing a storm of hunger within me. An announcement erupts from the speakers. Failing to understand the announcement, I opt to follow the crowd, which seems to have offboarded from the same plane, hoping to collect my big, brown suitcase.

I near the baggage collection area, butterflies flutter through my hungry stomach, dissipating my worries into the realms of nothingness as I spot my big, brown suitcase on the carousel. Standing on the sidelines by the carousel, I watch others pick up their luggage, and after a few failed attempts, I finally manage to grab her—my big, brown suitcase.

A wave of serenity breezes through me as I envelop Big Brown in my arms. I feel like I have just reunited with a long-lost childhood friend, and I stay in that moment, cherishing every second of it for a while. The smell lingering around Big Brown warps my mind back into the memories of my home—my mother's living room. The feeling of reassurance brims within me as I realize I'm not alone.

I can see my journey coming to an end – I'll soon be reunited with my friends. As I roam around for a bit, I find myself following the airport officer's instructions. He instructs me with his hand signal to trace others' footsteps to the immigration office. I have no clue what it means, but embracing courage, I walk forward.

A sense of confusion starts to ignite within me as I haven't prepared any flashcards for this step because I had no idea something like this existed. Gulping my rising anxiousness, I walk forward in front of the kiosk, and the immigration officers begin to ask me questions. I can't understand a single word that comes out of their mouths. As I stand there motionless in helplessness, I see the frustration and confusion blanketing the officers' faces. After struggling to communicate with me, they realize I cannot speak English or Hindi, so they stamp my passport and let me go.

"Phew! Another step has been taken and completed. Thank you, God!" I whisper to myself as I breathe out a sigh of relief.

My heart leaps with excitement; my soul brims with ecstasy as I follow others to the arrival gate, dragging my big, brown suitcase behind me. I stand on my tiptoes, looking above and past the crowd, as I try to locate my friends waiting for me at the arrival gate, but I don't see them. I hover my gaze through the unfamiliar faces, and panic starts to consume my thoughts. Worry suffocates my spirit since I can't find my friends anywhere.

Before I get imprisoned too deep in the cage of panic and fear, I see my angel in blue at a distance from me. The fog of worries starts to dissipate as she sees me and walks toward me.

"Are you all right?" she asks. Her *Farsi* words blanket my heart with peace and comfort as tears trickle down from my eyes. Joyfulness sprinkles onto my soul, and I express it with an anxious voice.

"Oh, I thought I had lost you for good. I'm so glad I found you again. I am worried. What if my friends don't show up? I don't know what to do if they don't come to pick me up."

"Do you have their phone number or address?" my angel asks in a consoling tone.

In these times, only the rich can afford the luxury of a phone, so I can't rely on this option since neither they nor I have a phone.

"No, I don't have anything," I reply. The embers of anxiousness spark within me as I realize how unprepared I am for this step in my journey. I peer into her eyes; she shines as the only ray of hope for me at the moment. I realize that I'm at her mercy if I want to reach out to my friends. Silence lingers between us for a moment as she ponders.

"Don't worry, dear. I will stay with you until you find your friends," she continues.

Comforting support imbues my heart as I begin to look around for my friends, searching every nook and cranny of that area while she patiently waits for me in the same spot. I feel the pinches of distress sending tremors of worry through my body. I can't find my friends anywhere. The stress of the angel leaving me behind burdens my mind. Marching back to her, I see her waiting for me, and I tell her that I can't find my friends anywhere.

Consoling me and telling me not to worry, she begins to point out Iranian people—since they have different facial features than the Indians—one by one, asking every time, "Is that your friend?" Looking carefully, I reply, "No."

With the rising stress and anxiousness, my mouth parches.

"Are you sure you don't have their address?" my angel asks again to see if I might remember something.

"No, I was sure they would be picking me up, so the thought of their address coming in handy never crossed my mind."

"Do you have anywhere else to go?"

"No," I reply as my hands tremble with the nervousness crawling through my body.

The thought of being in this foreign country with no knowledge of their culture and language sends cold shivers of fear through my spine. The light at the end of the tunnel of my journey starts to fade away as darkness swarms my path—when a bright ray of hope, my angel, pierces through it. Seeing my rising anxiety and shivering hands, my angel says, her words thriving with kindness, "Don't worry, I will take you to the Iranian consulate."

As her words sink into my soul, it feels as if someone poured ice-cold water on the burning, raging hot fire.

"But first, do you have Indian rupees?" she inquires.

"No, all I have is German marks," I reply.

"Let's go. I will take you to the bank to exchange money. You are going to need it."

Humbly, I follow her, assuring myself that I have no other option right now other than to trust her faithfully. There is no need or reason to doubt her intentions. As we walk out of the airport, the dazzling heat of Hyderabad pierces through my skin. It is a hot day compared to Shiraz, but at the same time, it illuminates the vibrant colors that this country is painted in. My angel calls for an auto-rickshaw as I stand beside her. The disruptive, hoarse noise from our ride abuses my ears as a yellow, three-wheeler vehicle with a driver seat in the front and two passenger seats in the back arrives in front of us.

As I examine this new vehicle, which I have never seen before, with amazement, I notice there are no doors—just a canopy to shield the passengers from the rain or the intense heat of the sun. Following my angel's lead, I sit in the back seat beside her, and slowly, yet steadily, we are on our way with Big Brown in front of our feet. Navigating through the streets as the driver zips between and through the vehicles and people, I let my gaze wander around my surroundings. The traffic comes from every direction like we are in a maze, and the loud noises of the horns reverberate through the streets. I feel disoriented.

People traveling by tricycles like rickshaws are pulled by skinny, sweaty men who seem like they are enjoying their ride while chewing on pan tobacco and spitting on the side of the street. *It is so loud and lively here*, I think. A large cow in the middle of the road is loitering, and the traffic stops for it without hesitation.

While I observe my surroundings, I tighten my grasp on the railing to support myself as I fear I might fall off the vehicle if I loosen my grip. With every turn the driver makes, we slip to one side and then the other. I tighten my grasp even more and glue myself to the seat. A cobbler sitting on a stool by the side of the road is busy repairing shoes. A tiny, old woman carries a big tray full of mangoes on her head as she approaches people to make a sale. My eyes twinkle as my surroundings become more and more vibrant, delighting my eyes.

Loud, Indian music blares in the streets, erupting from the shops and houses nearby, making me feel like everything has a life here. It feels so lively, unlike back in Iran, where listening to any kind of music is now considered a sin. My tired soul freshens up as it merges into the liveliness around it. Feelings of calmness take over me for a bit. I realize that I still have no idea where I'm going, but I'm completely in her hands.

We drive through a busy part of the city, which seems like a market, and she asks me if I'm hungry.

"Yes! Starving, to be exact. I couldn't eat anything on the plane because I was so worried and anxious," I reply, pouring honesty into my words.

Flourishing a smile on her face, she turns to the driver and says something in Hindi; I assume she asked him to take us to a restaurant. The driver zooms through a crowded area as I sit in the elevated back seat, circling my eyes through a crowd of black, dark heads moving, rushing in different directions.

The sight of the crowd, immersed in their chattering, captivates my consciousness as my mind warps back to the time of revolution in Iran, when people were on the streets chanting, "Down with the shah; Khomeini is our leader." As the world around me comes to a halt, I snap out of my déjà vu and notice that we are already in front of a restaurant in a busy marketplace.

Turning toward me, my angel asks, "Do you want chicken *biryani*?"

Pausing for a moment, I take my time translating and understanding her words by dissecting them. *OK, I know what chicken means*—morgh in Farsi—*and biryani might mean* fried. *Fried chicken sounds delicious and mouthwatering,* I think as happiness swirls in my eyes just by the thought of it, and pride fills me as I understand what she said.

"Yes, of course!" I answer.

Leaving me alone with the driver in the auto, Angel strides into the restaurant to get takeout for us. As soon as she disappears into the restaurant, fear pollutes my mind, making me feel unsafe as I begin to think, *What if the driver takes me somewhere to rape me or kill me?*

My eyes begin to widen in horror. I sit in my seat, frozen, praying for safety and trying my utmost to negate the negative thoughts.

My consciousness dissolves into my surroundings, and slowly, the fear begins to vanish. The hustle and bustle of the crowd around me, the bright colors reflecting the light of freedom in my eyes, and the aroma of the spices and coconut carve me out of my fearful thoughts. As people pass by, some stop to look at me, the foreigner. Some of them stride closer to me and start to touch my hand and my legs to look closely at my lighter skin color. The words of my mother echo in my mind as she always said that I was darker than the rest of my siblings. Having dark skin wasn't a good husband-finding feature!

This is nice, I never thought my color was anything interesting, I think, seeing that people are interested in my skin color. As the crowd gathers around me, the panhandlers and beggars make their way to me, too, asking for money and food. *"Amma amma, khaana dedo, paisay dedo."*

I can't understand what they are saying, but the driver yells and sends them away, *"Chalo, chalo."*

A burst of emotions—emotions of sadness—surge through me as I see the little children, the old man with leprosy, and the other hungry people begging for food. Yet, at the same time, an unknown fear crawls through me as I see what is in front of me. I have never experienced anything like this before. Needles of pain start to bury in my heart as I feel their pain down to my core.

Everything that unfolded and continues to unfold before me starts to make me feel like I'm living in a dream—a dream that has come to life in one day. *What an adventure I have signed myself into,* I whisper to myself while I anxiously wait for Angel to show up. As if my prayers bore fruit, from the corner of my eye, I see her walking toward the auto, looking like a fairy godmother, holding two big leaves in her hands.

Climbing into the auto, she makes herself comfortable in the seat beside me and hands me one of the leaves with food on it. I look closely at the rice with chicken pieces encrusted in spices resting on top. It looks nothing like fried chicken, but the aroma liberates my mind from worries, as it's heavenly. Averting my eyes from the leaf, I look at her with a puzzled expression evident in my eyes, not knowing what I'm supposed to do with the leaf.

"Where is the cutlery?" I ask her.

Embracing her beautiful Indian accent, she tilts her head side to side and replies in broken *Farsi*, "No. No, cutleries. You have to use your fingers."

As I stare at her in confusion, she starts to show me how to eat with my fingers. I can't hold back any longer as the aroma rising from the food is brimming with flavor, and my mouth starts watering. Learning from her, I mold a ball of rice with shreds of chicken in it and start eating. *Fire!* my first instincts scream as I feel a burning sensation flow through me from head to toe. As the spices explode in my mouth, I start to choke and cough, my eyes water, and my nose drips.

Instantly, she hands me a cup of water as she notices my body's reaction to spicy food. Minutes pass by as I strive and gasp for breath, but soon, I return to a normal state. So, this is my first experience with Indian food, and needless to say, I can't finish it.

My mind is anxiously busy with my next step and what lies ahead of me. My hunger subsides while I wait patiently for my companion to finish her lunch. After she's done, she directs the driver toward the Iranian consulate. Minutes later, the scenery around me starts to change as the Banjara Hills area nears where the consulate is located. All the noise erupting from the city vanishes as if we have entered into a totally different country. The clear, azure sky stretches over us as we steer through the clean roads guided by the fresh breeze of the tall trees stretching as far as the eye can see. Beautiful, luxurious mansions shadow the road, decorated with colorful flowers, majestic trees, neatly cut shrubs, and water landscape features. My eyes refuse to avert from the picturesque landscape before me, as even a glance at it induces a thrill, a rush of serenity within me.

Such a vast difference within a few minutes' drive from the poor section of the city, I think.

After a while, the auto stops in front of an architecturally beautiful building with plain, white walls. The geranium flowers bloom in front of the building—the sight of which reminds me of my home in Shiraz. As I stand in the shadow of the Iranian flag, I feel like I'm truly at home. *I have come a long way. It has been a journey filled with stress, yet full of adventures, and finally, I'm getting close to the end of a very tough day,* I think.

Mustering up my courage in my feet, I march into the consulate while Angel waits for me in the auto beside my big, brown suitcase. As I step inside, I notice the familiar pictures of Khomeini and other religious leaders hanging on the wall. As I linger my gaze over them, I realize that even though, until yesterday, the sight of those pictures reminded me of violence and injustice, today, seeing these pictures in the land of freedom … I truly feel liberated, as the fear of their rules and laws can't pin me down in this land.

Bringing my focus back to the matter at hand, I walk forward and ask the bearded man at the information desk if he knows someone named Safdar.

"No," he replies as he shakes his head. Not letting go of hope, I ask about Fadie and Sara.

"Sorry, I don't know them. You should go to the Iranian Muslim Students' Association and ask there. They might be able to help you," he explains, putting me on another path leading to my friends.

Dwelling in anxiousness, I walk back to the auto and explain to my angel what had happened. "Is that so?" she says. She turns to the driver and explains to him in Hindi. The driver seems to know of the students' association. Without wasting a single minute, we drive off to our new destination.

As we drive through the streets again, I look at Angel; I feel protected and safe beside her. Even though we have only known each other for a few hours, it feels like I have known her for an eternity.

After a short drive, we arrive at the Iranian Muslim Students' Association, and with a heavy heart, I turn toward my angel. She sees the worry in my eyes. I muster up the courage to say goodbye to her. She stops me and suggests that she wait in the auto holding Big Brown until I return and assure her that my problem is solved. A gust of immense gratitude rushes through me. I walk into the building, and instantly, a few men come to receive me at the entrance. Mumbling through my words, I ask them if they know my friends Fadie and Sara. They shake their heads, saying they don't.

Disappointment in my friends erupts within me, and I hopelessly ask the men if they know someone named Safdar. As they chatter with each other, a young man with a bushy beard steps forward, saying, "Yes, I know him." The flicker of hope reignites within me as happiness finds its way to my face, blooming a big smile on it. Hastily, I explain to him that Safdar is a student of my cousin, and I have received admission to this university through him.

"He usually comes here after his classes in the afternoon. You can wait here for him if you want," he replies.

"Yes, of course," I say excitedly, knowing I have no other choice.

With a surge of hope rushing through my veins, I run back to the auto to say goodbye to my angel in blue, gather my belongings, and pay my respects. In the short amount of time we spent together, I had formed a bond with her so deep that, as I bid her goodbye, tears flood my eyes. I hold her hands and hug her for so long, thanking her for all her help. I feel like I am short of words to express how grateful I am to find her on my path, and I hope she sees that in my expression. I wish I can meet her someday to repay her for her patience, her time, and her kindness.

As I pull my big, brown suitcase out of the auto and march toward the building, I look back to see her beautiful face one more time. Her kind eyes were beaming with joy. I wave at her with tears of thanks trickling down my cheeks.

While walking toward the building, a wave of sadness fills me as I realize this might be the last time I see my beloved angel in blue, but I know in my heart that she engraved within me a great lesson of giving without expecting. I am amazed at how she changed the old belief that you can't trust strangers in me. She taught me that there are angels in the guise of humans—even strangers. I wonder, if I wasn't so clear about my choice, would I ever have met the angel in blue? All through my journey, I was scared, but by meeting her, I learned I can ask for help, and if I am open to receiving, I will. I know now that help doesn't always speak my language, and it doesn't have to come from someone I know and am familiar with.

I feel like I entered a classroom, and my first teacher is my angel in blue. I am utterly grateful for her life lessons.

I walk inside the building with my big, brown suitcase rolling behind me. I see a few bearded men waiting for me inside. One of them starts to escort me to a room.

"Come this way, please," he says as he opens the door.

Entering the room right away, I notice a small bed neatly placed in the corner of the room. The words of that mature woman from the plane swirl in my mind as I can feel my face burning, turning red.

Are they going to rape me? What am I going to do? Should I run away before it's too late? Where will I go?

Countless thoughts start to flash through my mind as my face turns pale from horror like prey caught by hunters waiting to be devoured. My body trembles with fear as a faint, shivering voice escapes through my quivering lips, "OK."

Another man enters the room and brings my suitcase inside. Having Big Brown by my side brings me reassurance. A third man offers me some tea and biscuits, and they all leave the room. Trust replaces the fear in me quickly. I realize I am not lingering in a fearful state for too long. A wave of reassurance passes through me as I let out a great sigh of relief. I untie the knot securing my scarf under my chin and sit on the bed, exhausted and hungry. I haven't slept for two days. My tired body, drained of energy, aches. I start to sip from the cup of tea as I eat the biscuits. Tea and biscuits have never tasted so good. Relishing the moment of relief, I gaze out of the window where the landscape is illuminated by the brightness of the sun. I can see the beautiful, pink bougainvillea hanging over the walls, gating the houses, and the tall, dancing trees under the veil of a clear, blue sky.

Even though it's late autumn, everything is still lush green. The last time I walked on the streets of my beloved city, Shiraz, the wilted leaves in the fall season were scattered on the ground and crunching under my feet as a brisk breeze blew on my face. All I could see were mountains, desert, and sand at this time of the year, but it is all so different and beautiful in Hyderabad. I'm thousands of kilometers away from my family, and yet, at this moment, I feel like I'm very close to home.

I feel a freedom I never felt before—the kind of freedom you have when you dream that you are flying and soaring through the skies like a bird.

12

Trust

> The universe is filled with infinite possibilities and
> potential, if we only trust in its power to guide us.
> —DEEPAK CHOPRA

The canvas of the sky gets painted into a shade of crimson as the hours trickle by. I sit in that room, still waiting for Safdar to show up or for any news about him. As the sun dips into the western horizon, my heart sinks into a pool of impatience, raising ripples of worries that sweep through me.

What am I going to do if he doesn't show up? I ponder, creating a whirlpool of anxiousness in my heart. It feels like I have been waiting for a lifetime in this room. A knock reverberates through my consciousness, dissipating the storm of anxiousness as my eyes, filled with hope, linger over the door. With a faint creak, the door opens, and I see two men stride in.

One of them I know guided me toward my room when I sought shelter in the Iranian Muslim Students' Association. At his side stands a short, stubby man with his head covered with dark, curly hair and his lips shadowed by a big mustache. The first one introduces this short man as Safdar and leaves the room.

Excitement gushes through me while a tinge of surprise hovers in my gaze, as the Safdar before me looks nothing like I expected. He stands at the door with his head tilted downward and his gaze fixated on the floor. I can feel the breeze of serenity envelop my heart as his politeness and the respect he is showing me shroud me in a blanket of security.

From behind the veil of his mustache, Safdar opens his mouth and asks, "How are you doing, and how was your trip?"

Relief swarms my being as I relish the thought of being in the vicinity of a familiar person. Though I don't know him personally, he was recommended to me by my cousin, who had helped me get admission to the university. His presence gives me comfort. Knowing that everything will be all right now, I begin to narrate my journey from Shiraz to the Iranian Embassy in Banjara Hills.

I begin to pour the emotions and experiences I went through into my words as I explain to him how my friends abandoned me at the airport by not showing up. Embracing deep gratefulness, I relate the tale of my angel in blue, telling him how she aided me from the airport till I got here.

Listening intently to my story, Safdar nods as he says, "I know your friends."

His words infuse my essence with peace, which acts as a dressing for the wound that had stayed open to harsh winds since my friends did not come to get me at the airport. Even though I knew that Safdar might know them, since he helped them through the university admission process, a part of my heart worried, *What if he doesn't know them?*

The band-aid on my wounds rips off minutes later as he continues, "Unfortunately, I have no idea where they are."

The wound of worries ruptures again as I, again, stand at a juncture, not knowing which path will lead me to my friends.

"Can you ask about them from your friends?" I say, shrouding my hopelessness into the words of hope.

"I'm sorry, I don't know. Maybe Mahdy might know their whereabouts," Safdar says emphatically. Seeing through my petrified eyes, he continues, "I'll try."

I know he's just saying that to comfort me, yet a faint ray of hope shimmers through the darkness that started to surround my consciousness, but the fog of despair swirls around me as I drown in the fearfulness that I will never find my friends. No one knows them here, and I have no clue about their whereabouts. The emotions of hopelessness start to reflect on my face, turning red as I feel how desperately I am lost if I can't find my friends, my girls.

"Don't worry about it; I'll find you accommodation until you find your friends," Safdar assures me.

His gesture of kindness brings relief to my terrified senses, while it sends tremors of shock through the base of my beliefs—a guy helping a woman. I was brought up in an environment where I was constantly taught not to trust a strange man, but here he is—a strange man helping me find a place to live. Searching through the alternate options in my head, I accept his gesture as I can't find any other path beyond his help. As I sit there, I peek into my soul, instilling words of confidence in it, reassuring myself to be open to new possibilities since I'm not the same old, shackled person. I'm liberated.

As I follow Safdar, my heart brims with gratefulness. First, there was my angel in blue, who helped me in every way, and now, I have found another angel who's sacrificing their time for my sake. As I relish the breeze of relief brewing inside me, a tinge of fear mixes in it—the pessimistic beliefs with which I was brought up cloud my mind, filling it with thoughts like, *Is this real? Life cannot be just filled with angels … Is this another trap that I'm falling into?*

This time, I shun the aura of pessimism and walk on the only path I have with courage, embracing the unknown as if I'm soaring through the skies, tearing through the clouds, not knowing where I'll land.

"Wait here. I'll let you know when the auto arrives," Safdar says as he prepares to march toward the road, leaving me to stand near the exit to the students' association with my big, brown suitcase.

"OK, but where are we going?" I ask.

"To my house. It's near Banjara Hills so that you can rest there," he replies and marches off to arrange our transportation.

I stand in my place, constantly assuring myself that everything will be fine, just go with the flow, while my eyes linger over Safdar's back as he calls over an auto—another three-wheeler taxi—as if it were just waiting for him. Returning to me, Safdar picks up my suitcase and loads it up in the auto while I sit in one corner. I jolt with shock as Safdar sits beside me; my heart starts thumping, remembering I'm not supposed to touch a man, and I edge away from him and push myself into the corner while I wonder, *What is his plan?*

While navigating through the honks and noise from the hordes of black-haired people with the aroma of coconut oil soaring, the noise of my fearful thoughts echoes loudly within me while the roars of my surroundings are dulled. Our auto finally arrives at our destination. Stepping off the auto and unloading my companion—my big, brown suitcase—I hesitantly trace Safdar's steps as he leads the way.

While my heart quivers with the fear, I whisper to myself, "Have faith that he's a decent person. He won't harm you; it's just your anxieties speaking. What's the worst that could happen? Nothing. Did I have any other option? No. I must place my trust in him. I must trust myself, and whatever comes my way, I'll manage to take care of myself and my safety. After all, I've traveled this far alone."

Drenching my quivering heart in the words of consolation and courage, I commit myself to taking a leap of faith and facing my fate head-on.

After a minute of walking, I find myself standing in front of a small bachelor house as Safdar unlocks the door. Accepting his invitation, I step inside, and warm, homely winds sweep my face. As I allow my gaze to wander around, I see a single room in the house with a bed placed in the corner, a little kitchenette on the side, and a compact, little bathroom. Safdar shows me around the tiny house and says, "Get comfortable here."

Instantly, the pessimistic part of my mind soars a thought in my head: *What is he going to do? Is he going to stay here, too?* My mind quivers faintly with the rising fear inside me.

"You are welcome to have anything from the fridge if you want. Take showers when you want. I'll stay with my friends until you find your friends," Safdar explains as he gestures with his hands toward the amenities in the house, all with a warm smile on his face.

Relief blows away the remnants of pessimism inside me as I thank God he's leaving. A deep gratefulness spreads its wings within me as I relish the kindness of these angels who have helped and are helping me.

"Thank you!" I bring my heartfelt gratefulness to my tongue as I slightly bow my head to him in appreciation.

Safdar leaves; I let down my guard and relax enough to be more aware of my stomach's growling from hunger. Making my way to the fridge, I satisfy my hunger with the meal placed in the fridge. Tiredness and exhaustion crawl through my body. I take a shower and wash off the residues of my worries and the pollution from the streets before I allow myself to hit the bed. Drowsiness takes my body to the realm of dreams as I fall asleep quickly.

Jolting from my slumber, I roam my eyes around as specks of streetlights shimmer across the room from the gap in curtains, illuminating my way to the washroom. As I stride back into the room, my head still in a state of drowsiness, my eyes catch a glimpse of something in the shadowed part of the room. Removing the peel of sleepiness from my eyes, I focus, and shivers of fear travel through my spine as I gaze at a skull placed on the shelf along with scraps of bones.

A shriek escapes my mouth as I utter, "Oh my God! What did I do to myself? He probably killed this person and put their skull on display." All the worries, the fears, the pessimistic thoughts I had shunned away, rush back into my existence as I stand there, motionless, quivering in fear—fear for my life.

My heart thumps wildly, trying to break out of its cage of ribs. Imbued with horror, I bind my soul as I sit on the bed with my knees barricading my chest and my lips constantly in motion, chanting prayers for the morning sun to rise and for someone to come and rescue me. The horror, the fear, and the trauma warp my consciousness to the time when I was six years old. My mom sent me to buy yogurt from the nearby corner store. At that time, the shopkeepers made yogurt in their homes, stored it in a tray, scooped the yogurt into the customers' bowls, and handed it over.

So, as I extended the bowl my mom gave me toward him, the shopkeeper grabbed my hand, skimmed his hand forward to my shoulder, and started to work his hand down. My senses tingled with the bells of warning, screaming at me that something was wrong. I pulled my hand away, grabbed the bowl, and ran toward my home without any yogurt. When I got home, my mom saw my pale face, as if blood had been sucked out of it, and asked about the empty bowl of yogurt. Gasping for breath, I narrated to her the event that took place, but she could do nothing except ban me from going there again.

That same helplessness and fear crawl through me as I worry that no one will be able to help me this time if something happens. Time trickles through the chasm of fear and loneliness as the golden aura of the sun scatters across my face, but my eyes, drenched in horror, refuse to avert from the skull as I tilt back and forth.

Moments later, Safdar knocks at the door, opens the door, and before he comes in, he calls, "Good morning, Parvin. I'm here," and walks in through the front door. His footsteps ring the alarms of fear in my heart, as if the angel of death has arrived. As he walks into the room, he notices me sitting, cuddled up on the bed, with fright written all over my face.

"What's happened!?" he inquires, shards of worry etched in his voice.

"I-It's just this …" I stutter as I point my quivering finger toward the shelf. "What's this on your shelf?"

"Oh, I'm a medical student. This was a project I was working on," he explains as he rubs the back of his head and lightly chuckles.

All my fears seep out from the sigh of relief I take. The thoughts of Safdar being a serial killer dissipate into nothingness as I finally take a breath of solace.

Season to Reap

The greatest glory in living lies not in never
failing but in rising every time we fail.
—NELSON MANDELA

The withering heat of the sun drenches my shrouded body as I stand at the precipice of my dream—my freedom. I raise my eyes from the ground and focus on two wide, metal gates in front of me. My soul relishes the manifestation of my long-held dream as my mind wobbles at my current reality. As I allow the excitement to rise up within me, I find I cannot be completely exhilarated. Part of my soul misses the warmth, the scent, and the protection of my family, while the other part relishes the breeze of independence. A rush of emotions gushes through me as my mind tries to grasp this new feeling, this new sensation of standing on Indian soil—a foreign territory. I'm not used to this.

As I assimilate this strange sensation in my bones, I hold my head up high, arch my shoulders back, and imbuing the essence of courage in my eyes, I gaze beyond the horizons of the wide, metal gate. Flashes of memories pass through my mind as I remember the day I stood in front of the American embassy's tall, iron gates. While I reflect on my past self, the dreadful emotions of that day—the day I thought I would forever be bound in the shackles of absurd laws, the day I thought I would forever be a hostage in my home country—swirl through me as I remember the hope of being a free woman vanishing from my life gush through me.

Gulping down the bitter memories, I redirect my consciousness to my surroundings and submerge myself in the serenity that lingers in the air. It's so quiet here. The lullabies of the birds chirping induce peace in my soul as the swishing sound of the gentle breeze blankets me. As the fragments of my being dissolve into the tranquility, a light of realization illuminates my heart and I assure myself that this is my new beginning, my brand-new start to life.

Tall trees are swaying with the wind; lush, green patches of land are a blissful sight for my eyes after seeing the dry deserts of Shiraz for decades. This is the land that, even in my dreams, I never thought I would land foot on—but here I am, with my feet planted on its soil. A ripple of contentment passes through me. Navigating through the maze of hardships, my life took an unexpected turn for finding myself here is not too far from what I had planned. This is not America, but in the few days I have been here, I'm beginning to feel at home.

With my mind absorbing the surroundings, I lose track of time as my eyes stare at the gates aimlessly, while my mind hovers through the lands of memories and dreams—past and present. I jolt in my spot as my mind carves itself out of its thoughts when Safdar taps on my shoulder.

"Where are you? Where's your mind? We have to go in," he says.

"Sorry, I was just dreaming. I'm ready. Let's go," I reply apologetically.

"Where is the doorbell?" I inquire as I roam my eyes over the gate confusedly.

"There's no doorbell," Safdar replies as he pushes open the gate and waits inside, gesturing for me to go inside first.

I embrace courage in my center, lift my big, brown suitcase over the step, and tread inside. With each step, my dream becomes closer and my heart turns ecstatic. The heat penetrates through my manteau and *hijab*, making my body drenched in sweat. Suffocation makes me gasp for breath as I shake the front of my manteau with my hand to let the air swirl inside and cool down. With the sun shimmering above my head, the suffocation rises as I want to tear my *hijab* off my head and let the open air embrace me, but the fear of the revolutionary guards, embedded deep in my soul, crawls through my veins. I hesitate to take my *hijab* off in case they have been following me.

In the midst of December, the heat warps my consciousness to the summer season of Shiraz. My heart drowns in nostalgia as I remember my mom spreading a blanket under a sour-orange tree and cutting some fresh watermelon for us to enjoy under the shade. The memory of those times makes my heart quiver as I crave my mom's presence beside me. I miss her. I wonder how she would react if she saw me here in this foreign country. Would she believe I managed to make it here all alone? Even I'm still in awe. Even I can't believe I'm finally here.

As I shuffle through my thoughts, my footsteps come to a halt, and my eyes wander through my surroundings. A serene smile paints across my face as I find myself drowning in the mesmerizing greenery around me. My head turns from side to side, guided by my eyes as they try to grasp the picturesque landscape in front of them—tall, ancient trees shadowing the pathway, green bushes fencing the lush, green grass of the garden. In every nook of the land before me, beauty thrives. *This must be what heaven looks like,* I think.

After a while, my eyes turn to where my footsteps point—a tall mansion, a jewel of architecture, blurred in the distance as a winding pathway stretches toward it. In front of this mansion, my entity feels miniscule. The decorative, red sand is sprinkled over the pathway, reminding me of the mountainside in Shiraz, where our family often went for picnics. I played catch and hide-and-seek in the sand with my cousins. Lost in the thrill of the moment, we chased each other until my mom would call me.

"Parvin! I just washed these clothes. Look, you are full of dust," she would yell.

My mind relives those pleasant memories until I realize that my mind, my soul, was imprisoned by the absurd laws after the revolution. The laws of our house had shackled my mindset, making me feel like I was living in jail, and I had to break through that.

Abstaining the taste of sour memories from ruining my present, I liberate myself from the shackles of the past. As I stride forward, I see a man with a bindi painted on his forehead readjusting the white fencing stones around the pathway. The green grass in the garden stretches as far as the eye can see. This is so unlike Iran, where tall walls surround the yards for privacy. Since the revolution, simple privacy has not been enough, so people are installing two- to three-meter-high barbed wires on top of their walls for security. This is because robbers began to run wild as social order broke down, and the aspect of feeling safe had been stolen from their lives. By the time I left the country, it wasn't safe anymore to leave the house without leaving someone behind for security. Here, the only boundary needed is tall trees—an aspect of freedom that had been robbed from us in Iran.

Submerged in silence, dwelling on my thoughts, I follow Safdar as we tread closer and closer to the building. In the veil of the echo of my shallow footsteps, a faint crunching sound of my big, brown suitcase, which I am dragging behind me, hangs in the air. As we near the mansion, the sight of a fountain surrounded by a range of vibrant, colorful flowers instills within a feeling as if I'm walking into a movie scene.

Savoring the liberating feeling swirling inside me, I breathe in the fresh misty air from the water fountain, and my eyes inspect the mansion in front of me—white stones are etched in its walls and two tall pillars with captivating engravings on them stand erect beside giant, wooden double doors, encapsulating the building in a majestic aura. The wide, stone steps lead me to the wooden gate. I jolt my suitcase over them and stop at the top for a few minutes to catch my breath. With each breath, I think, *Can this all be true? I'm standing so many kilometers away from the place I call home, yet I feel so safe here.*

With my energy rejuvenated, I fix my scarf and straighten my manteau. Waiting for the next step, I hesitantly look at Safdar, holding the door hammer in my hand. He nods and winks. I know now that is his way of showing approval. Heaving out a sigh, I shroud my heart in courage as I knock thrice. Each knock reverberates within me the memory of my dad. This is how he used to knock, and it was a sign for me to know he was home. As the echoes of the knock submerge in my soul, a part of me misses him, while I remind myself that if he were still alive, I would never have been allowed to make it here.

After waiting for a while, the door creaks open, revealing a young woman decorated in a red-and-gold sari with her long, braided hair parted into two sections, one resting on each shoulder, reveals herself. My eyes hover over her ensemble as they try to capture fully the incredible vibrance of the woman in them. Greeting her, Safdar says something to her in English, and she extends her hand to shake Safdar's hand. As they shake their hands, a gasp escapes my mouth as, to my eyes, to my imprisoned mindset, it was taboo after the revolution for a man to touch a woman in such a casual manner.

If she were in Iran, she would have been imprisoned and tortured for this, I conclude to myself as I cover my mouth with my hands. I can feel my face turning red as the heat of embarrassment spreads through it. My cheeks begin to flush profusely. Averting my eyes from them, I tilt my head down and bury my gaze on the floor to hide the thoughts traversing through my mind.

A hand appears in front of my lowered eyes as I lift my head and see the woman has extended her hand to shake mine.

"My name is Amina," she announces slowly but loudly.

Returning her greeting, I shake her hand as I say, "Hello, my name is Parvin. I room here," while I point inside the building. I march inside, following Amina and Safdar, and arrive at the foyer.

At that moment, Safdar explains something to her and then turns to me and says, "Wait here."

As I wait in my spot, Safdar and Amina disappear into one of the rooms while I wait by the foyer. With them gone, I immerse myself in observing the internal décor of the house. I notice a circular stairway winding along the walls with a wooden sculpture of a naked woman situated at its base. Astounded by the sculpture, I wander my gaze around and notice another one placed a few steps higher and a third one placed right behind me. A rush of emotions of embarrassment surges through me as my mind whispers to me, *Oh, I hope Safdar didn't see them. It would be too embarrassing for a man to see them.*

Curiosity spins through me as I notice a bunch of doors around the foyer, and I wonder where they might lead. During my curious visual journey, I notice a door slightly open. With my interest peaking inside me, I stretch my neck and peer into the room. My eyes widen in surprise as I see a tall woman dressed in a white sari, sitting elegantly on a beautiful bed as if she were a queen sitting on her throne, with two men sitting on the floor in front of her. This queen-like woman is treated just like men are treated back home after the revolution—royalty.

As I hear a few noises approaching from the room where Safdar and Amina disappeared, I jolt back into my spot and see Safdar walking up to me with a big smile stretched across his face.

"The flat is yours. You can move in now. Just pay the rent they asked for. You've got money on you, right?" he asks.

A flurry of emotions flows through me as my ears twitch, unable to fathom that I'm finally here at the gate of my dreams. A smile complimenting my emotions paints over my face as I excitedly reply.

"Really? I can move in. I knew it! That's why I wanted to bring my suitcase with me. Yes, yes, I have cash."

Words spurt out of my mouth, as I'm still in awe that this is really happening. Hastily, I scavenge through my handbag while Amina stands beside me with a smile. I pull out the rent money from my handbag and hand it over to Safdar to count, as I'm still not familiar with the Indian rupees. Like a wobbly, excited, little chickadee on its first attempt to fly, I ask, "Is it right?"

"Yes, it is right," he says, and he hands the cash back to me so I can hand it over to Amina. The burden of all my struggles begins to vanish into nothingness. I feel light, while pride fills my chest.

"*Shukriya,*" she expresses her gratitude in her language and leads me up to the spiraling stairs. While I trace her footsteps, Safdar carries my big, brown suitcase up the staircase.

"What do you have in here? Rocks? It's so heavy," he jokes.

A light chuckle escapes my mouth as I blush. "I'm sorry. Here, let me carry it."

"No, no, I was just joking," he replies lightheartedly.

As I march up the unending, elevated stairs, my mind warps to the time when I stood at the top of the staircase of the plane leaving for India and was captivated by the last sight of my homeland in my eyes. Sorrowness spreads through me as my pent-up emotions trickle through my eyes. I think, *Will I ever see my family again? Is this a goodbye forever?* I wipe away my tears with the back of my hand as I knock on the doors of my dream, filling the flask of my soul with joy as butterflies flutter in my chest—more with each step.

Shortly, I ascend onto the second floor and catch up with Amina. White walls with mahogany railings surround me. I follow Amina as she walks toward one of the three doors beside a spacious sitting area and comes to a halt in front of one of them. My heart thumps ferociously in my chest as I see the light of my dream shimmering over me. Opening the door, she says something, and Safdar translates it for me.

"Here it is: your room," he says, and he brings in my suitcase. My eyes, drenched with curiosity, aimlessly wander from one nook of the room to the other, my mind in a daze as I stand on the other side of the door of my dreams. Before I can say anything, Amina places the room key in my hand, and they both leave.

A storm of emotions swirls through me as I feel the briskness of the air lingering in the room. My arms stretch wide open as if I'm about to hug the room, my dream. The essence of my emotions trickles down from my eyes as I wipe away my tears and put my purse on the twin bed, the only furniture in the room. My soul quivers with bliss as my heart leaps the boundaries of joy, puppeteering my body into twirling in the open space with my head tilted back like a Sufi dancer. The cold air from the ceiling fan teases my face, instilling a tinge of freshness in me and carving out the tiredness etched in my bones.

The sunlight disperses into the room from the windows, reflecting from the white-painted doors and walls, brightening up the room. While I submerge my gaze into the intricacies of my room, I notice a balcony attached to it. Stepping forward, with excitement rushing through my veins, I march onto the balcony and behold the lavish view of the front of the building emerging below. I skim my eyes over the landscape before me and notice a few stray dogs roaming aimlessly, searching for food. The sight of them sparks within me the memory of revolution—the times when little children were scouring desperately through the markets, searching for food in the trash. The claw of empathy grips my heart as I flinch and walk back inside.

I bask in the light of my success—the fruit of all my struggles—as I skim my hand over the walls of my room like a painter feeling their blank canvas before they begin painting. The specks of excitement linger in my heart as I imagine the decorations and furnishings I can do in my room. I feel like I have wings to fly—wings of freedom.

Treading toward the only window, facing the back of the house, I open the shutters to see the huge terrace fenced by neatly carved, white stone railings. The sun shines brightly through the window, impairing my vision of the backyard. With my curiosity rising, I raise myself on my toes and poke my head out, but with the sunlight shining in my eyes, my vision is still hazy. With a sigh of defeat, I give up and march back to my big, brown suitcase and caress it gently. I can feel the scratches on her body and see her worn-down wheels with empathy flickering in my eyes. The sight of scars on her body reminds me of my struggles as I pour my feelings into my words, "We have been through a lot. You are one tough suitcase," I whisper to her.

I envelop her in my arms as I sit cross-legged on the floor and reminisce over the long and tiring journey. Being here, sitting in this warm sun with this brisk air enveloping my tired body … it all feels like a miracle, but it isn't. I'm here. Tears of happiness, sadness, tiredness, ecstasy … encapsulating all my emotions, tears trace down my cheeks and fall on the big, brown suitcase.

Amid the fog of emotions, I open the suitcase's zipper and flip open the top. My eyes rest on the photo album placed neatly on top of everything else. With a weak smile, I flip it open, and on the first page is the picture of my mom, shrouded in her chador, sitting beside Uncle Reza.

This must have been taken when I was very young, I ponder while I caress my hand over my mom's face as sadness floods through me. She is covered from head to toe, but her face shows she is young. Mom disliked taking pictures without *hijab* in case a man saw the picture—remnants of my argument with her swirl through my mind as I remember.

"But *Māmān*, it's only a picture," I argued.

"You don't understand. Even a picture without *hijab* can send you to hell," she retorted.

I let out a light chuckle as tears trickle down from my eyes. I flip through the pages and see my sister Arie with her husband and three children in the picture. She looks like she was around twenty-five when this picture was taken. She got married at the age of fourteen and already had her first child when she was fifteen. Peeking into the past as I sit here, enveloped in freedom, I let out a deep sigh of relief.

"Thank God I escaped having to go through what she did," I say to myself.

A flood of emotions gushes through me as I flip through each page, unlocking a concealed memory with each page turn. As I unroll the scroll of memories, I see the picture of my friend Fahi and myself. The hair on the back of my neck stands as I see our red eyes, remembering the horrors of that day. We were on our way back home from the Ministry of Education and were blinded by the tear gas. Until then, being blinded by tear gas always seemed mythical to me, but that day, fear deepened its claws in my heart.

We ran away from the area, partially blinded by the gas as it stung our eyes with each passing minute.

"We didn't do anything wrong. Why are they doing this to us?" I shouted.

"I don't know. Let's just go before we get in trouble." Fahi coughed.

When we reached her home, her dad thought we looked funny and clicked this picture of us with our eyes bloodshot from the tear gas. As I sit here, I feel liberated for not having to worry about such things anymore. The taints of the past are slowly washing away as I spend time in this serene area. With sadness filling the flask of my soul, I close the book, as I don't have the courage to live through those memories again, and shove the album under the bed.

Getting up from my spot, I see another door to the left of the balcony, which I haven't investigated. I push open the door with curiosity, quelling the sadness in my heart, and there it was, my own bathroom and kitchen. I wondered where it would be! It's spacious, almost the size of my room, with a table stretching across the wall in one corner, supporting a stove and buffet beside it. The sunlight scattered through this space from the large window beside the shower.

"I guess this is my bathroom and kitchen at the same time," I say to myself.

My excitement knows no limits, as I realize that everything in this room is mine and mine alone. Exploring the realm of my dreams, I gaze at the single door to the left of the window.

I wonder where this leads to, I ponder.

Marching forward, I hold the door by the handle and pull. Nothing— it's jammed. I refuse to give up and pull at it harder and harder again. After numerous tries, the door opens with force, and I fall back onto the ground. The pain vanishes in an instant as I see a large terrace connecting the entire width of the building, illuminated under the sunlight. The sight before me is breathtaking, as the landscape beyond consists of rocky hills scattered through it, followed by a small lake behind the building.

I lean against the white stone railing, resting my elbows on the handrail as I dissolve my gaze into the marvels of nature before me—the glistening water of the lake under the gentle sunlight, the forest shadowing a patch of the area, the tinge of freshness in the air as I inhale. As my consciousness submerges in the flowing water of the lake, I reflect on my journey. Throbs of pain make my heart quiver as I realize I might not see my family ever again.

I miss their laughter, their jokes, and their warmth. I miss the language, the people, and the culture I was raised in, but I remind myself that if I had stayed back, I would have been a servant of some man for my entire life, acquiescing to whatever they had chosen for me. If, at any point, I had failed to follow the rules in public, I would have been rotting in jail, to be tortured, interrogated, or worse.

I wonder how many girls feel like I did, but the shackles of fear hold them back from taking action. As the chirps of the birds, hums of the wind, and the flow of water sync in my mind, I ponder over the things I learned from my long and tiring journey: If something doesn't feel right, I can always change my path, my direction, and alter my beliefs to where I feel comfortable. It's possible to carve my own path, to make things the way I want them to be. I hold the reins of my life and feel powerful being in control of my future.

A smile flourishes on my face as I embrace my reality and skim my hand over my *hijab*. With one hand, I hold it in place, while with the other, I loosen the knot under my chin. The scroll of memories unfolds as I slowly take it off my head—the revolution, the guards, the laws, the jail, the torture ... the fear of unwrapping it. Slowly, everything fades away, as I take off my *hijab*.

The wind caresses my head as the grip around my *hijab* loosens, and it flies away. Seeing it carried away on the waves of wind, I feel like it carries with it all my burdens. I feel more liberated and freer than ever.

Voicing the liberating emotions, I exclaim, *"Man, azadam, azad"* (Finally, I'm free)!

About the Author

Parvin Kolahdooz is an Iranian-born Canadian memoirist, a certified Integral master coach, and a lover of nature. With a deep understanding of the complexities of human experience, Parvin's memoirs offer profound insights into the human condition. Through her writing, she shares her story of overcoming adversity and finding freedom, inspiring readers to navigate their challenges with courage and resilience. As a coach, Parvin is dedicated to helping individuals unlock their full potential and navigate life's transitions with grace and confidence. Her compassionate approach and unwavering commitment to personal growth make her a trusted mentor and guide for those seeking transformation and fulfillment in their lives. Explore more about Parvin's work by visiting her website, www. innerpotentialcoaching.com.

Acknowledgments

My late mother, Fatemeh, was brave and was an amazing role model for me. Her strength has always been the wind beneath my wings.

My husband, Andrew, has always been there for me and supported me every step of the way, reviewing versions of this book as it evolved and giving me the feedback I needed.

My children, Arash and Ida, provided unconditional, loving support and believed in me.

My teacher, Alison Wearing, gave me the tools to write this book.

My friend, Manijeh, has been a transparent friend and given endless support.

My angel in her blue sari, whose real name I never got to know: If you are reading this book, please contact me. Thank you for being my selfless angel.

Finally, my friend, the late Safdar, and my cousin Mahdy were the two men who opened the path for me.